Magic Bullet

101 Recipes

You Can Make In 10 Seconds Or Less

www.HomelandHousewares.com

Welcome

At Homeland Housewares, our primary mission is to ***make your life easier***. Our recipe selection process is based on two key principals: ease of preparation and fantastic taste. That's why we kitchen-test ***every*** Magic Bullet recipe ourselves to be sure it's easy, delicious, and a breeze to clean up. And since we're not professional chefs, we don't expect you to be either, so we make sure every recipe is straightforward and simple to follow. We cook up these recipes in our very own homes and try them out on our families, friends and neighbors. It's because of this "grassroots" process that we ***know*** you are going to love all 101 of these lip-smacking, and easy to make recipes. It wouldn't be in this book if we didn't enjoy making it, and thoroughly enjoy eating it!

In this volume, we share even more 10-second-or-less dip, appetizer, cocktail and meal recipes, plus we've added several exciting ***new sections*** including ***Dressings***, ***Sauces***, ***Marinades***, ***Quick Breads*** and ***Side Dishes***.

The ***Dressings***, ***Sauces and Marinades*** sections open up a whole new door of Magic Bullet possibilities. You'll see how, with a few common household ingredients, and without any chopping, dicing or stirring, you can whip up healthy, tasty, preservative-free dressings, sauces and marinades in the blink of an eye. We share our favorites including zesty Spicy Avacado Dressing, tangy Sweet and Sour Sauce, hearty Bullet Barbeque Sauce, spicy Mexican Fajita Marinade and many, many more. They are all very easy to make and absolutely delicious.

Everyone loves fresh, warm bread and biscuits, so that's why we're so excited about the ***Quick Breads and Biscuits*** section. When using the Magic Bullet, favorites like Pumpkin Bread and Parmesan-Herb Biscuits are effortless to create, and a snap to clean up. No more bowls, spoons, mixers and mess. With these simple Magic Bullet recipes, you just need your Bullet and a loaf pan or cookie sheet, and you're in business.

Welcome

No meal is complete without a little something on the side, so we've created a ***Side Dish*** section that includes some of our all-time favorites. How about some creamy, flavorful Twice-Baked Potatoes or spicy Sesame Noodles to round out your favorite main dish? All the side dishes are simply irresistible, and can be made in just seconds.

We hope you enjoy every one of the 101 Magic Bullet recipes. But remember, the Magic Bullet is so quick and easy, we encourage you to experiment with alternate ingredients and your own favorite recipes. Use our tried-and-true recipes as a launching pad to create your own Magic Bullet masterpieces. Bon Appetite!

The Icons Used in This Book

For your convenience we've created a series of icons so, in a glance, you can quickly learn a lot about a recipe or technique. Here is a legend of the symbols used throughout the Magic Bullet 101 Recipes book.

Use the ***Flat Blade*** attachment

Use the ***Cross Blade*** attachment

Fat-Free

Vegetarian

Kid-Friendly

Contains alcohol, act responsibly

Travels well

Caution

Table of Contents

Table of Contents

Table of Contents

Table of Contents

Dips

From cool and creamy Clam Dip to warm and zesty Cheese Dip, these mind-blowing, simple party dip recipes will not only have your guests applauding, they'll be done in seconds so you'll be mingling instead of chopping, dicing and stirring in the kitchen. It's party time!

10-Second Tzatziki

You know that awesome relish-like sauce that comes on gyros and falafel plates? Now you can make it at home in just seconds. This creamy Greek dip is light and refreshing, perfect for any time of day.

1 cup plain yogurt
Sprig or 2 of dill (optional)
1/2 a de-seeded English cucumber (or 1 regular cucumber)
3 cloves of garlic
Pepper to taste

First... Add 1/2 of a de-seeded, unpeeled English cucumber to the ***Tall Cup*** and **Pulse** 3-4 times with the ***Cross Blade*** until chopped up but still chunky.
Next... Screw the ***Steamer Top*** (the smallest holes) onto the cup containing the cucumber and drain out the excess liquid.
Then... Add all the other ingredients into the ***Tall Cup*** with the cucumber.
Finally... Twist on the ***Cross Blade*** and **Pulse** until you achieve a blended but textured consistency.

Some of us like our Tzatziki as thick and chunky as possible, and we got the best chunkiness by using English – often called Hothouse – cucumbers. You can find them in the produce section near the regular cucumbers. Also, if you scoop out the seeds and soft flesh from the inside of either type of cucumber, you get chunkier results. For super chunky tzatziki, you can even stir in diced cucumber after you've mixed all the ingredients.

Traditional tzatziki is a little chunky, and is best served chilled with triangles of pita bread or as a vegetable dip. In Greece, it's a common side to meat dishes. Create your own gyro by adding leftover meats into a pita and pour a little tzatziki over the top. Delicious!

Fat-Free Version Use fat-free free yogurt instead, and this is a tasty, fat-free free dip.

Ridiculously Quick Roasted Red Pepper Dip

This mouth-watering, zesty dip is perfect for any occasion. Day or night, summer through winter, there will always be a crowd around this dip!

Splash of balsamic vinegar (optional)
1/2 cup of sour cream
2 cloves of garlic
1/2 cup of roasted red peppers (from jar)
Pinch of thyme

First... Place all ingredients, in the order they are listed, into the ***Short Cup***.
Then... Twist on the ***Cross Blade*** and blend until smooth.

Roasted red peppers can be found in the pickle and olive area of most grocery stores.

Serving Suggestion: Serve cold or at room temperature with wedges of pita bread, or small slices of French bread. You can also use this as a delicious veggie dip. Serve it with baby carrots, celery sticks and your other favorite vegetables.

Dips

Tips: ***Fat-Free version*** Use fat-free yogurt instead of sour cream, and this is a tasty and healthy dip.
Red pepper sauce Add one cup of chicken (or vegetable) broth to make a

sauce perfect for pouring over chicken or fish.
Red pepper soup Add 2 cups of chicken broth to make a zesty, flavorful soup – a great way to use any dip leftovers.

7-Second Summer Salsa   

Feeling a little sassy? Try this twist on traditional salsa and watch your friends and family flock around this tasty concoction.

- 4 oz. Picanté sauce
- 6-8 cherry tomatoes (or 2 Roma or 1 regular-sized)
- 1/4 whole zucchini
- 1/4 whole cucumber
- 1 slice of onion (optional)

First... Place all ingredients, in the order they are listed, into the ***Tall Cup***.
Then... Twist on the ***Cross Blade*** and **Pulse** 5-8 times until you've achieved a blended but chunky consistency.

Notes: We like our salsa chunky. If you do too, don't over-do the **Pulsing**. When you pour your fresh salsa in a bowl, you may notice the power of the Magic Bullet has made it a little foamy. The foam does settle after a few minutes, but to quickly remove it, simply lay a paper towel on top of the salsa and gently blot.

Serve with tortilla chips, as a taco topping, or as a zesty topping for fish, chicken or beef.

Super Quick Clam Dip 

Watch your guests come out of their shell to enjoy this party dip favorite. It's a cool and creamy flavor sensation that practically makes itself!

- 4 oz. cream cheese
- 1 6.5 oz. can of minced clams
- 1 thin slice of onion (or half a boiler onion, about 2 tsp)
- 2 tsp. Worcestershire sauce
- A few drops Tabasco™ pepper sauce to taste
- 1 Tbs. mayonnaise
- 2 Sprigs parsley (no stem)

First... Add all of the ingredients to the ***Tall Cup*** and mix with the ***Cross Blade*** until well blended.
Then... Twist on a ***Stay Fresh Re-sealable Lid*** and chill for about 2 hours before serving.

Serve with crackers or slices of crusty French bread.

Before You Can Say Olive Tapenade 

This savory spread is perfect for cocktail parties. Its lusty flavor is a sure palate pleaser.

- 1 cup pitted black olives
- 2-3 cloves garlic
- 1/3 cup anchovies (rinsed)
- 1 Tbs. capers
- 1/2 cup extra virgin olive oil

First... Rinse canned anchovies in hot water to reduce salt.
Then... Add all the ingredients, in the order they are listed, into the ***Tall Cup***.
Finally... Twist on the ***Cross Blade*** and **Pulse** 5-8 times until the ingredients achieve a slightly textured consistency.

Serving Suggestion This olive spread is delicious when served with sliced Italian or French bread or with crackers. It can also be used as a decadent sandwich condiment, or as an accompaniment to fish or poultry.

Lickety Split Cheese Dip   

Creamy, chunky, warm cheese dip – serve it with tortilla chips, or slices of crusty Italian bread. One of the finer things in life!

- 8 oz. cheddar (or Velveeta™) cheese
- 1/4 cup salsa (mild, medium or hot)
- 1-2 Tbs. milk
- 1-2 sprigs fresh cilantro
- 1/4 jalapeño pepper (optional)

First... Add all of the ingredients to the ***Short Cup*** and **Pulse** with the ***Cross Blade*** 5 or 6 times, or until the ingredients are mixed together.
Then... Twist off the blade and twist on a ***Steamer Top***. Microwave the ingredients for 2-3 minutes on medium heat, or until cheese is melted and dip is warm throughout.
Finally... Twist the ***Cross Blade*** back on and **Pulse** a few more times. Serve immediately.

Appetizers

You'll look like a culinary school graduate when you whip up any of these quick and easy, delicious appetizers. Impress your friends and family with fabulous party time favorites like Crunchy Crab Cakes, Devilishly Fast Deviled Eggs and luscious Stuffed Mushrooms. And you're the only one that needs to know that every one of these delicacies is prepared in just seconds!

Suddenly Stuffed Mushrooms

What is it that makes stuffed mushrooms so special? We don't know for sure, but we do know these puppies will be gone before you can blink an eye. Do your guests a favor and make two batches. Scrumptious!

10-12 large mushrooms
1/4 cup ricotta cheese
1/2 cup spinach
1 oz. square of parmesan
1 clove of garlic
1/4 cup onion
Splash of chicken (or vegetable) broth

First ... Pre-heat the oven to 350 degrees.
Next ... Pop the stems off of the mushrooms making an area for the stuffing in the mushroom top.
Then ... Add all in the ingredients except for the mushrooms into the small cup and twist on the ***Cross Blade***.
Next ... **Pulse** until the consistency is chopped well but not quite smooth.
Finally ... Spoon the mixed ingredients into the mushroom tops and cook on a baking sheet for 15-20 minutes.

This recipe fills about 10-12 mushrooms. If you want to make more, simply double the ingredients.

Tips

This recipe is the standard stuffed mushroom recipe. Feel free to add crab meat, crumbled bacon, lobster, whatever your heart desires, and you'll have scrumptious stuffed mushrooms that will have your guests swooning!

In the Blink of an Eye Bruschetta   

This simple, elegant, tomato-basil "relish" served on toasted bread rounds melts in the mouth without compromising the waistline. This Italian classic will be instantly devoured. That's amore!

- 8-10 cherry tomatoes or 1 regular-sized tomato (about a 1/4 cup)
- 4 sprigs basil (or more if you want)
- 1-2 boiler onions or 1/4 of a regular sized onion (about 1/4 cup)
- 2 cloves garlic
- 1/2 Tbs. olive oil (optional)

First ... Add all the ingredients, in the order they are listed, into the ***Short Cup***.

Then ... Twist on the ***Cross Blade*** and **Pulse** 5-8 times until you reach the desired consistency.

Notes: Bruschetta is delicious as a fine puree or as a chunky spread.

Serving Suggestion: Use your Magic Bullet to make a paste of butter and garlic. Spread that on sliced crusty Italian bread and lightly toast. Add a little bruschetta to the top of each slice and serve. You can also serve it as a dip with sliced Italian or French bread.

Couldn't Be Quicker Crab Cakes 

Who can say no to a crab cake? This particular recipe is so good; it may put the state of Maryland out of business. These crunchy, delicious crab cakes are a perfect appetizer for any party, or even as a main course.

2 sprigs fresh parsley
Pinch dry mustard (can use more if desired)
1/4 tsp. Worcestershire sauce
1 egg
1/2 Tbs. mayonnaise
1/4 cup fresh bread crumbs (see tip)
1 can cooked crab meat (drained)
Salt and pepper to taste

First ... Add all ingredients EXCEPT crab to the ***Tall Cup***.
Then ... **Pulse** a few times with the ***Cross Blade*** until the ingredients are blended but still chunky.
Next... Open the cup, add the can of drained crab meat and twist on the ***Stay-Fresh Re-sealable Lid***. Simply shake the cup like a cocktail mixer 6-8 times, or until you can see the crab has mixed with the other ingredients.
Then... At medium temperature, heat 4 tablespoons of olive oil in a skillet while forming the crab mixture into patties (it will make 2 meal-sized cakes, 6 medium-sized cakes and about 12 bite-size).
Finally... Fry until golden brown on both sides (3-4 minutes per side).

Notes: Rolling the crab mixture into tight balls and then flattening into patties helps to hold the best shape during the frying process. Try not to flip the cakes too early; the less flipping, the less chance of breakage.

Serve on a platter with wedges of lime. These crab cakes go hand and hand with margaritas. Sheer bliss!

Tips: **No breadcrumbs?** No worries. Make your own by placing a piece of bread, a little parmesan and some Italian spices in the ***Short Cup***, and **Pulse** a few times with the ***Cross Blade*** (even stale bread works!). Or, throw in a few croutons instead.

Devilishly Fast Deviled Eggs

This easy to make (and even easier to eat) American classic is a party time staple. Whip up a batch and watch them disappear. Eggs-ellent!

12 eggs, hard-boiled
1/3 cup mayonnaise
4 Tbs. mustard
4 Tbs. sweet pickle relish
Salt and pepper
Hot red pepper sauce to taste (optional)
Paprika, for garnish

First … Hard-boil the eggs.
Then … Peel and cut eggs in half lengthwise, and remove the yolks. Place the yolks in the ***Tall Cup*** and the egg white "cups" on a serving plate.
Next … Add all the other ingredients to the yolks in the ***Tall Cup*** and mix with the ***Cross Blade*** until smooth.
Then … Sample the mixture, adding a little more mayo or mustard depending on your taste. Once it's to your liking, spoon the mixture into the egg white "cups".
Finally … Sprinkle the tops with paprika.

Chill and serve cold. If you don't like to add relish to your deviled eggs, feel free to omit it, or replace it with capers.

Quick-n-Kickin' Shrimp (or Scallops) Sauté

When you decide to make this killer shrimp sauté, be prepared to give the recipe to every guest there. Whether you serve it over pasta, or in bowls with bread for dipping, you and your guests are going to love this spicy, festive, flavorful seasoned shrimp sauté. Enjoy!

2 Tbs. olive oil
1-2 boiler onions or 1/4 of a regular sized onion (about 1/4 cup)
3 Roma tomatoes or 2 regular-sized tomatoes (about one cup)
2 Tbs. salt (optional)
1/2 tsp. crushed red pepper (or more, or less)
1/4 tsp. black pepper
16 oz. bag of frozen shrimp (scallops or fish)
1 cup dry white wine
1 cup water

First … Add everything except the shrimp, wine and water into the ***Tall Cup*** and twist on the ***Cross Blade***. (You may have to cut the tomatoes to make them fit.)
Then … **Pulse** 4 – 5 times. (You want the consistency to remain a little textured.)
Next … Pour the ***Tall Cup*** contents into a large sauce pan and cook over medium high heat for 8 minutes
Then … Pour the wine and water into the pan and bring to a boil.
Finally … Reduce heat to medum and add shrimp.
Cover and cook for 15 minutes or until done.

Serve over hot pasta or in small bowls with bread for dipping.

Substitute scallops or whole pieces of fish for the shrimp.

Appetizers

8-Second Crock-Pot Hot Wings

These spicy wings are perfect for any occasion. They are so easy to make and so tasty to eat. The sauce takes just seconds to make, then you pour it over your wings and cook in the crock-pot. Mmm...mmm! Dig in and enjoy!

2 Tbs. olive oil
2-5 garlic cloves
3-4 boiler onions (1 regular-sized onion)
1-4 jalapeño peppers
4 lbs. chicken wings
2 cups vinegar-based barbecue sauce

First ... Rinse the chicken wings in cold water and place them in a crock-pot.
Then ... Place all the other ingredients in the ***Tall Cup*** (if you're using a larger onion, you'll have to quarter it) and blend with the ***Cross Blade*** until smooth and creamy.
Next ... Pour the mixture over the wings and stir.
Finally ... Cover the crock-pot and cook on preferred setting (high about 4 hours, low 8-10 hours, or until cooked).

Use 4 jalapeños only if you're into "burn-your-face-off" wings. If not, reduce the amount of jalapeño according to your taste.

Tips

A vinegar-based barbecue sauce will list vinegar before tomato on the ingredient list, so check the ingredients. Many popular brands of barbecue sauce are vinegar-based.

6-Second Crabby Cukes 

Snappy, snazzy, and delicious – crunchy cucumber rounds are topped with a creamy, zesty crab dip, and are as appealing to look at as they are to eat. Your guests will be "Oohing!" and "Ahhing!" over the display. That's 6 seconds very well spent!

- 1/2 cup mayonnaise
- 2-3 tsp. prepared horseradish
- 1 tsp. Dijon mustard
- 1 tsp. Worcestershire sauce
- 1 can (4.25-ounce) of crabmeat
- 1 large unpeeled English (Hothouse) cucumber, cut crosswise into 8-10 thin slices (about 1/4-inch-thick slices)
- 8 pimento-stuffed green olives, sliced

First ... Add mayonnaise, horseradish, mustard, and Worcestershire sauce to the ***Tall Cup*** and **Pulse** with the ***Cross Blade*** until blended but still textured.
Next... Twist off the ***Cross Blade*** and add the crabmeat. Do not blend the contents. Twist on the ***Stay-Fresh Re-sealable Lid*** and shake the ***Tall Cup*** until the crab mixes in with the other ingredients.
Then... Place the mixture in the refrigerator for 30 minutes.
Finally... When you're ready to serve, arrange the cucumber slices in a single layer on a serving tray and spoon 1 tablespoon of crabmeat mixture onto each cucumber slice, garnishing each one with an olive slice.
Serve immediately.

Super Easy Bleu Cheese Bites

Crunchy, warm and cheesy: Your guests will gobble up these yummy little bread bites before you can say “bleu cheese!”

- 1/4 cup butter or margarine
- 3 oz. bleu cheese
- 2 8 oz. cans of refrigerator biscuits.

First ... Open the canned biscuits and cut each one into quarters. Set aside.
Then ... Add the butter and bleu cheese to the ***Short Cup*** and microwave for one minute (or until melted).
Next ... Twist on the ***Flat Blade*** and blend the butter and cheese until smooth.
Finally ... Dip each biscuit piece in butter/cheese mixture and bake on a greased cookie sheet at 450 degrees for 10 to 12 minutes.
Serve immediately.

Frozen Cocktails

Frozen cocktails are what makes the Magic Bullet the "Ultimate Party Machine", because only the Magic Bullet comes with the one-of-a-kind *Party Mugs*. You can prepare and serve drinks in the same mug, so making a different type of frozen party drink for everybody is easy. Enjoy this fabulous frozen drinks section chock full of recipes including Hawaiian Lava Flows, and a Homeland Housewares original, The Pretty Blue Sledgehammer.

Frozen Banana Daiquiri

This rich, delicious, frosty cocktail is perfect on those hot days. Throw in an umbrella, close your eyes and you'll swear you're on vacation in Bermuda.

2 oz. light rum
1/2 oz. triple sec
1 oz. lime juice
1/2 tsp. sugar
1 banana
Ice

First … Add the banana and fill the ***Party Mug*** or ***Tall Cup*** with ice.
Then … Pour in all of the ingredients.
Finally … Blend with the ***Cross Blade*** until smooth.

To make an **Easy Banana Daiquiri**: just mix pre-made daiquiri mix with the rum, banana and ice.

The Twee Chee

We gave the traditional Chi Chi a little twist and a little kick. This tasty, tropical, refreshing cocktail is perfect for poolside parties and afternoon soirées. The combination of sweet and tart is a tropical treat for the taste buds.

1 oz. vodka
1 oz. coconut rum
1 oz. cream of coconut
1/2 cup pineapple juice
1/2 cup half and half
Ice

First … Fill the ***Party Mug*** or ***Tall Cup*** with ice.
Then … Pour in all the ingredients.
Finally … Blend with the ***Cross Blade*** until smooth.

Clockwork Orange 

After a few of these, your friends are going to seem like they're straight out of a Kubrick film! This fruity concoction is light and tasty.

2 oz. Citrus Vodka
1/4 cup frozen peaches
1/4 cup mango juice
1/4 cup pineapple juice
Ice

First … Add the frozen fruits and fill the rest of the ***Party Mug*** or ***Tall Cup*** with ice.
Then … Pour in all the ingredients.
Finally … Blend with the ***Cross Blade*** until smooth.

Lava Flow

Have a little bit of Hawaii without the long flight. This fruity colada drink is a delicious, refreshing favorite that "erupts" with strawberry lava. It's sure to have your taste buds saying "Mahalo!"

1 oz. light rum
1 oz. Malibu Rum™
2 oz. strawberries
1 banana
2 oz. pineapple juice
2 oz. coconut cream
Ice

First … Fill the ***Party Mug*** or ***Tall Cup*** with ice, banana, coconut cream, Malibu rum and pineapple juice and blend with the ***Cross Blade***.
Then … In the ***Short Cup***, add rum and strawberries and blend with the ***Cross Blade***.
Next … Pour the rum/strawberry mix into the bottom of a hurricane glass then pour in the banana mixture.
Now … Using a spoon, drag the strawberry mixture up through the banana mixture, to create a pink stripe or two.

Green-Eyed Monster 

Whoever is standing next to you is going to be green with envy if they don't have one of these in their hand. This tasty, sweet and sour melon drink is perfect for brunches, luncheons and poolside parties.

2 oz. melon liqueur
6 oz. sour mix
1/2 tsp. sugar
Ice

First ... Fill the ***Party Mug***, or ***Tall Cup*** with ice.
Then ... Pour in all of the ingredients.
Finally ... Blend with the ***Cross Blade*** until smooth.

To make a ***Green-Eyed Mondo Monster***, add 2 oz. of vodka before blending.

Frozen Cocktails

Pretty Blue Sledgehammer

This sweet, tasty, pretty drink was actually invented by the president of Homeland Housewares. It's perfect for poolside festivities, but be careful, this one packs a whollup!

2 oz. sour mix
2 oz. Blue Curacao™
1/2 oz. vodka
1/2 oz. gin
1/2 oz. light rum
Splash of lemon-lime soda
Ice

First ... Fill the ***Party Mug***, or ***Tall Cup*** with ice.
Then ... Pour in all of the ingredients.
Finally ... Blend with the ***Cross Blade*** until smooth.

Cool Beans

You'll be licking your lips when you taste this rich and creamy, coffee-flavored frozen cocktail. This deliciously satisfying, all-occasion drink is a sure crowd pleaser.

2 oz. Kahlua™ (or coffee brandy)
2 oz. vodka
2 oz. cream or milk
Ice

First ... Fill the ***Party Mug*** or ***Tall Cup*** halfway with ice.
Then ... Pour in all of the ingredients.
Finally ... Blend with the ***Cross Blade*** until smooth.

To make a ***Feliz NaviDaddio*** replace the cream with eggnog.

Roll Out The Barrel 

A day without root beer is like a day without sunshine. Why suffer? Go ahead and try this refreshingly delicious grown-up version of a root beer float.

2 oz. vodka
2 oz. root beer schnapps
2 oz. heavy cream
2 oz. cola
Ice

First … Fill the ***Party Mug*** or ***Tall Cup*** with ice
Then … Pour in all of the ingredients.
Finally … Blend with the ***Cross Blade*** until smooth.

This last cocktail isn't frozen, but it is soooo good we wouldn't dream of leaving it out. Enjoy!

Bullet Bloody Mary

What's brunch without a Bloody Mary? It's just a late breakfast. The power of the Magic Bullet distributes the ingredients in such a way that every sip of this rich and tasty Bloody Mary is bursting with flavor. This "from scratch" recipe will make you a local legend.

6 oz. tomato or vegetable juice
2-3 oz. vodka
1/2 tsp. (or more) horseradish
2-3 peppercorns
Dash celery salt
Splash of Worcestershire
Tabasco™ sauce to taste (several drops)

First ... Add all ingredients to the ***Tall Cup***.
Then ... Blend with the ***Cross Blade*** until smooth.
Finally ... Pour into a hurricane glass and add ice.

Feel free to substitute Clamato™ juice instead of tomato or vegetable.

Serving Suggestion: Bloody Maries are typically served with a celery stalk. Other tasty add-ins are marinated string beans, green olives, cocktail onions, or anything else you can think of. Plus, you can add celery salt to the rim of the glass by pouring celery salt onto a plate, swiping a lemon wedge around the glasses' rim to dampen it, then twisting the rim back and forth in the celery salt to coat.

Breakfasts

With the Magic Bullet, the most important meal of the day is so easy you wouldn't dream of skipping it. And forget about the "donut and granola bar" days – now you can prepare delicious breakfasts in less time than it takes to brew a pot of coffee. Imagine simple, no-mess breakfasts like fresh-from-the-oven Ham and Cheese Quiche, or luscious Veggie Cream Cheese Schmear that takes less time to prepare than toasting the bread to swipe it on. All these delectable breakfasts can be prepared in seconds, and are ready to devour in minutes. Now that's waking up on the right side of the bed!

10-Second Tomato-Cheese Frittata

Real men don't eat quiche, they make frittatas! Man, woman and child will all love this hearty, flavorful egg dish. Whip one up in seconds and by the time you're dressed, you've got a breakfast you'll be drooling over.

1 Tbs. butter
1/2-1 boiler onion, or a generous slice of a regular onion
4-5 cherry tomatoes, or 1/2 a regular-sized tomato
(about 1/4 cup)
4 eggs
1/4 tsp. seasoned salt (optional)
1/4 tsp. oregano
2 Tbs. milk
2 oz. cheddar cheese
3 sprigs fresh parsley

First ... Add butter and onions to the ***Tall Cup*** and **Pulse** with the ***Cross Blade*** 4-6 times.
Then ... Microwave on high until the butter melts (about 30 seconds).
Next ... Add the remaining ingredients and **Pulse** with the ***Cross Blade*** until the ingredients have blended to a chunky consistency.
Then ... Pour into an 8 x 8 greased baking dish.
Finally ... Bake at 350° for 25-35 minutes, or until set.

Frittatas make a lovely breakfast, lunch or dinner. Sliced fruit is a great breakfast side dish and a mixed green salad is perfect for lunch or dinner.

Ham and Cheese Pie

Hot, gooey, ham and cheese on the bottom, flakey crust on the top, pie. What more needs to be said? Just throw a few ingredients in the Magic Bullet and by the time the gang meets around the kitchen table, you'll have a dish that is sure to become a family favorite.

- 6 oz. ham or 1 cup of diced ham (8 - 10 deli slices)
- 6 oz. cheddar cheese (1 cup shredded, 8 -10 deli slices)
- 1 cup milk
- 3 eggs
- 3/4 cup Bisquick™ mix
- 1/3 cup mayonnaise
- 1 Tbs. mustard

First … Preheat the oven to 350 degrees.
Then … If you're using chunk or cubed ham and cheese, add the ham and cheese to the ***Tall Cup*** and **Pulse** with the ***Cross Blade*** until you've achieved a spreadable, but chunky consistency.
Next … Spread the ham and cheese along the bottom of a lightly greased 9-inch pie pan. If using deli cuts, lay them into the bottom of the pan as is.
Then … Place all the other ingredients in the ***Blender Attachment*** and blend together until smooth.
Finally … Pour the mixture over the top of the ham and cheese and bake for 30 to 40 minutes, or until you can stab the center with a toothpick and it comes out clean.

Crazy Quick Banana Cream Crepes

Start your morning off with a little slice of heaven. Each light and airy crepe is filled with delectable banana cream filling. Voila! – Five-star decadence in the comfort of your own home.

For Crepes:

1 cup water
1 cup whole milk
2 cups all-purpose flour
2 Tbs. sugar
1/2 tsp. salt
3 large eggs
4 Tbs. melted butter

For the Banana Cream Filling:

1 banana (the riper the better)
8 oz of whipping cream
1/2 tsp. vanilla
Pinch of cinnamon

Crepes:

First ... Combine all of the ingredients in the Magic Bullet ***Blender Attachment*** and use the ***Cross Blade*** to blend until smooth.
Then ... Heat a lightly greased 7-inch nonstick frying pan over moderately high heat.
Next ... Pour enough batter to cover the bottom of the pan, and cook the batter for about 1 1/2 minutes (until lightly browned). Then flip the crepe over with a rubber spatula and cook the reverse side until lightly browned (about one minute).
Then ... Transfer to a plate and repeat the process with the remaining batter.

Banana Cream Filling:
First … Fill the ***Tall Cup*** halfway with heavy cream and whip it with the ***Flat Blade*** (you'll hear when it's done).
Then … Add the banana, cinnamon and vanilla to the whipped cream, and blend with ***Cross Blade*** until smooth.

To serve:
First … Coat each crepe with 1 tablespoon banana filling.
Then … Roll into a "log".
Finally … Dust with confectioner's sugar or cocoa powder (or both!).

For the best crepe formation, blend the batter and refrigerate, covered, for at least 2 hours or overnight.

In-An-Instant Cream Cheese Schmear

Ahh…whipped cream cheese – a fabulous, easy breakfast, brunch, or lunch delicacy. Bring on the bagels!

1 cup cream cheese
Small splash of milk

Pick one (or a few) Popular Add-Ins

Chives
Sun dried tomatoes
Dill
Red Onion
Scallions
Basil
Lox
Pineapple
Roasted Red Pepper (from jar)

First … Add the cream cheese, milk and your favorite "Add-Ins" in to the ***Tall Cup***.
Then … Blend with the ***Cross Blade*** until smooth.
Serve.

Serving Suggestion: Cream cheese schmears are most often served with bagels. Another tasty cream cheese treat is Stuffed Celery. Just fill the center of a few celery stalks with cream cheese and cut into bite-size pieces. Or simply use the schmear as a Veggie Dip.

Tips: ***To Make Cream Cheese Cukes:*** Follow the instructions above then swipe cream cheese onto cucumber rounds (cut a cucumber into 1/4-inch thick slices) and chill until serving time. A kid favorite!

Ham and Cheese Quickie Quiche

How about a nice Quiche on the lips? That's what you're going to get when you prepare this scrumptious dish. So good, it will become a household legend.

1 unbaked 9-inch refrigerator pie shell
4.5 oz. (1 cup) cooked ham
2.5 oz. (1/2 cup) cheddar cheese
2 Tbs. all-purpose flour
Freshly ground black pepper to taste
4 eggs
1 cup half-and-half cream
1/2 cup packed chopped fresh spinach (optional)
1 (4 oz.) can mushrooms, drained (optional)

First … Preheat the oven to 350 degrees, fit the pie shell into a 9-inch lightly greased pie plate then heat the shell for about 10 minutes.
Then … Add all the other ingredients to the ***Blender Attachment*** and **Pulse** with the ***Cross Blade*** 2-3 times, so the ingredients are blended, but still textured.
Finally … Pour the mixture into the pie shell and bake for 45-55 minutes until filling is set and the top is golden.

Serving Suggestion

To make a Veggie Quiche: Omit the ham and cheese and add 1/4 cup of defrosted frozen broccoli, 2 boiler onions and 5-6 cherry tomatoes. Feel free to experiment with your favorite veggies.

Breakfasts

To make Bacon, Mushroom, Tomato Quiche: Omit the ham, cheese and spinach and add 1/2 cup (about 6 -8 slices) of cooked bacon and 6-8 cherry tomatoes.

Soups

You can have fresh wholesome soup in less time than it takes to heat up canned soup. Hooray! Forget the can opener, water, pot, pan, spoon and bowl. With the Magic Bullet, your favorite veggies, and *Short Cup,* in just seconds you'll have fresh, delicious soup that's ready to eat, or travel! Simply twist on the *Stay-Fresh Re-sealable Lid* and your soup is ready to go to the office, school, or wherever you want to enjoy this healthy, nutritious meal. Just heat it up and eat it up. Magnificent!

Speedy Carrot Soup

What's up doc? Creamy, tasty carrot soup in seconds that even Bugs would approve!

- 1 cup baby carrots
- 1 clove garlic
- 1/2 cup chicken stock
- 1/3 cup cream (or milk or non-fat yogurt)

First ... Add carrots, garlic and chicken stock to the ***Tall Cup***.
Next ... Twist on the ***Steamer Top*** and microwave for 2-3 minutes, until the carrots are soft.
Then ... Open cup and add cream (milk or non-fat yogurt).
Finally ... Twist on ***Cross Blade*** and blend until you have a smooth soup-like consistency.

Notes: This recipe is for one bowl, or 2 cups, of soup. For more servings, just multiply each ingredient by the number of servings you want to create. For more than 2 servings, use the ***Blender Attachment***.

Tips: ***Fat-Free version*** Use fat-free plain yogurt or skim milk instead of cream.
Vegetarian version Use vegetable broth instead of chicken broth to create a vegetarian version.

Pumpkin Soup with Ginger and Coconut Milk

Ready to create a culinary sensation in less time than it takes to find your can opener? Try this gourmet blend of ingredients and you'll be loving life. Go ahead and have some more, you deserve it.

1 cup canned pumpkin flesh
1 clove garlic
1/2 cup chicken stock
1/3 cup coconut milk
Pinch of ginger

First … Add pumpkin, garlic, ginger and chicken stock to the ***Tall Cup***.
Next … Twist on the ***Steamer Top*** and microwave for 2-3 minutes, until the pumpkin is soft.
Then … Open the cup and add the coconut milk.
Finally … Twist on ***Cross Blade*** and blend until you have a smooth soup-like consistency.

This recipe is for one bowl, or 2 cups, of soup. For more servings, just multiply each ingredient by the number of servings you want to create. For more than 2 servings, use the ***Blender Attachment***.

Tips: ***Vegetarian version*** Use vegetable broth instead of chicken broth to create a vegetarian version.

7-Second Squash Soup

You're going to squash every can of soup you have after you try this homemade, fresh and tasty delight.

1 cup squash
1 clove garlic
1/2 cup chicken stock
1/3 cup cream (or milk or non-fat yogurt)

First ... Add squash, garlic and chicken stock to the ***Tall Cup***.
Next ... Twist on the ***Steamer Top*** and microwave for 2-3 minutes, until the squash is soft.
Then ... Open cup and add cream.
Finally ... Twist on ***Cross Blade*** and blend until you have a smooth soup-like consistency.

Notes: This recipe is for one bowl, or 2 cups, of soup. For more servings, just multiply each ingredient by the number of servings you want to create. For more than 2 servings, use the ***Blender Attachment***.

Tips: ***Fat-Free version*** Use fat-free plain yogurt or skim milk instead of cream.
Vegetarian version Use vegetable broth instead of chicken broth to create a vegetarian version.

Behold! Black Bean Soup

This hearty, satisfying soup is a full meal. This recipe is sure to become your newest comfort food favorite. And surprise! It's healthy! So dig in, guilt-free!

1 15 oz. can black beans
1/4 cup onion
1-2 cloves garlic
1/4 cup roasted red peppers (from jar)
2 cups chicken broth
2 Tbs. balsamic vinegar
Cayenne pepper to taste (optional)

First ... Place all ingredients, in the order they are listed, into the ***Blender Attachment***.
Next ... Twist on the ***Cross Blade*** and **Pulse** 5-8 times until you reach the desired consistency.

Finally … Twist off the ***Cross Blade***, twist on the ***Steamer Top*** and microwave for 2 minutes or until hot.

Notes Roasted red peppers can be found in the pickle and olive area of most grocery stores. This recipe makes about 3 bowls of soup.

Tips ***Fat-Free version*** Use fat-free chicken broth for a delicious, hearty fat-free lunch or dinner.
Vegetarian version Use vegetable broth instead of chicken broth to create a vegetarian version.

Asparagus Cream Soup

You'll have no soup to spare when you whip up this fantastically flavorful, hearty soup. It's simply breathtaking.

- 1 cup asparagus tips
- 1 clove garlic
- 1/2 cup chicken stock
- 1/3 cup cream (or milk or non-fat yogurt)

First … Add asparagus, garlic and chicken stock to the ***Tall Cup***.
Next … Twist on the ***Steamer Top*** and microwave for 2-3 minutes, until the asparagus is soft.
Then … Open cup and add cream.
Finally … Twist on ***Cross Blade*** and blend until you have a smooth soup-like consistency.

Notes This recipe is for one bowl, or 2 cups, of soup. For more servings, just multiply each ingredient by the number of servings you want to create. For more than 2 servings, use the ***Blender Attachment***.

Soups

Make the most of your asparagus Snap the end off each stalk with your hands. The asparagus will break-off at exactly the point you want to use.

Fat-Free version Use fat-free plain yogurt or skim milk instead of cream.

Vegetarian version Use vegetable broth instead of chicken broth to create a vegetarian version.

It's Ready Already Red Pepper Soup

This is a creamy, zesty, flavor sensation. Once you try this soup, you can't stop thinking about it. You'll want it again and again!

- 1/2 cup sour cream
- 2 cloves garlic
- 2 cups chicken broth
- Splash of balsamic vinegar (optional)
- 1 cup roasted red peppers (from jar)
- Pinch of thyme

First … Place all ingredients, in the order they are listed, into the ***Blender Attachment***.
Then … Twist on the ***Cross Blade*** and blend until smooth.

Notes

Roasted red peppers can be found in the pickle and olive area of most grocery stores. This recipe makes about 3 bowls of soup.

Fat-Free version Use fat-free chicken broth for a delicious, hearty fat-free lunch or dinner.

Vegetarian version Use vegetable broth instead of chicken broth to create a vegetarian version.

Marinades

Any good cook will tell you, a meat dish is only as good as its marinade. This exciting new *Magic Bullet Marinades* section will show you how a few seconds of effort and a few simple ingredients can turn ho-hum, tough cuts of meat into delectable, tender creations that will melt in your mouth.

Tips for Marinating

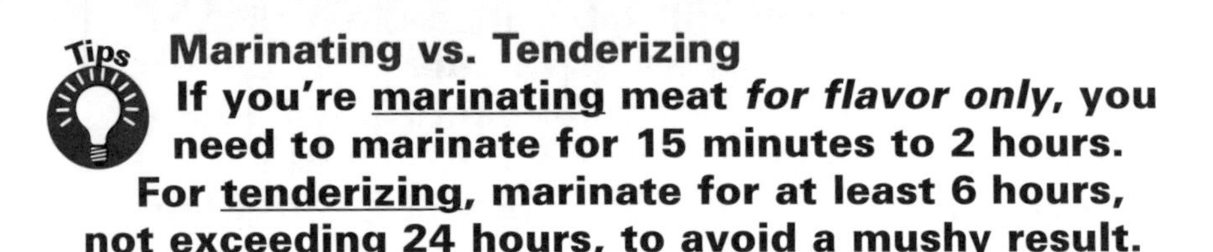

Tips

Marinating vs. Tenderizing

If you're <u>marinating</u> meat *for flavor only,* you need to marinate for 15 minutes to 2 hours. For <u>tenderizing</u>, marinate for at least 6 hours, not exceeding 24 hours, to avoid a mushy result.

Safety Guidelines

Never save marinade that has come in contact with raw meat. If a marinade is to be used later for basting or served as a sauce, reserve a portion of it before adding the meat or fish. Always marinate in the refrigerator, never at room temperature, and marinate in a food-safe plastic bag, plastic container, or glass dish.

Variations

We encourage you to vary the ingredients in these marinades, but make sure your recipe includes wine, vinegar, or lemon juice. These acidic liquids are necessary to break down the meats' connective tissues for thorough marinating.

Fish Marinade

Go fish! It's easy to add more fish to your diet when it tastes this amazing! Zesty, light and satisfying, this fish entrée is a gourmet experience with this simple to make marinade.

- 2 cups white (Chablis) wine
- 2 Tbs. lemon juice
- 2 tsp. salt
- 2 Tbs. Creole mustard
- 1/2 tsp. cayenne pepper (or red pepper flakes)

First ... Add all the ingredients to the ***Blender Attachment*** and blend with the ***Cross Blade*** until smooth.
Then ... Pour 1/2 of the marinade over the meat of your choice and marinate for at least 15 minutes.
Finally ... Save the remaining marinade for basting as you cook the fish.

Once you've tried this on fish, you may want to marinate everything in it. Go for it! It's fantastic on chicken, pork chops, or beef.

Lime – Ginger Marinade 

This zesty blend with a citrus tang is just perfect for grilling, baking or sautéing. It's a tantalizing treat for the taste buds, indeed!

- 6 Tbs. lime juice
- 3 Tbs. honey
- 2 Tbs. rice wine vinegar
- 2 Tbs. olive oil
- 2-3 sprigs of cilantro
- 1/2 to 1-inch slice ginger root
- 1/4 tsp. red pepper flakes

First ... Add all the ingredients to the ***Tall Cup*** and blend with the ***Cross Blade*** until smooth.
Then ... Pour over the meat of your choice and marinate for at least 15 minutes.

This marinade is just perfect for chicken, shrimp, steak, fish, you name it.

Steak Marinade 

You better stake your claim on your piece of steak when you marinate with this blend, because the meat will be gone before you can say "come and get it!"

1 cup olive oil
1/2 cup red or white wine (or 1/4 cup lemon juice)
2 Tbs. soy sauce
3 cloves garlic
2 Tbs. freshly parsley (or your favorite fresh herb)
1 tsp. Italian seasoning
1/2 tsp. black pepper
Red peppercorns (optional)
1 Tbs. Worcestershire sauce
1 tsp. sugar

First … Add all the ingredients to the ***Tall Cup*** and blend with the ***Cross Blade*** until smooth.
Then … Pour over the meat of your choice and marinate for at least 15 minutes.

Make a double batch and save 1/4 marinade for basting. Then heat the remaining sauce, and serve as a fabulous twist on au jus.

5-Second Mexican Fajita Marinade 

Spice up your chicken, steak and fish with this super-fast, flavorful, do-it-yourself Mexican favorite. Muy bien!

- 5 cloves garlic
- 1/3 cup soy sauce
- 1/3 cup red wine vinegar
- 1/2 cup olive oil
- 1/2 to 1 tsp. of red pepper flakes
- Sprig of cilantro

First ... Add all the ingredients to the ***Tall Cup*** and blend with the ***Cross Blade*** until smooth.
Then ... Pour over the meat of your choice and marinate for at least 15 minutes.

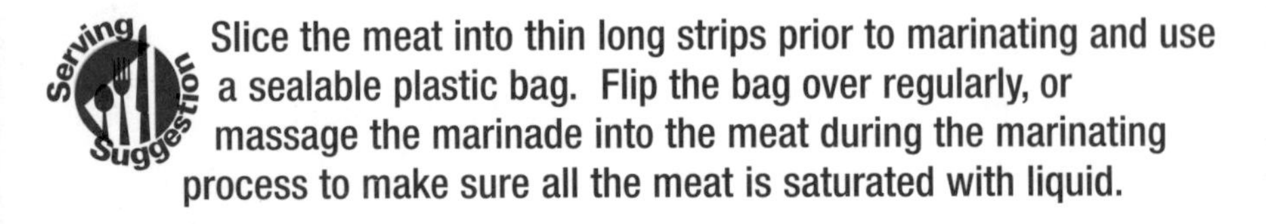

Slice the meat into thin long strips prior to marinating and use a sealable plastic bag. Flip the bag over regularly, or massage the marinade into the meat during the marinating process to make sure all the meat is saturated with liquid.

Fajitas need to be tender to taste their very best. If the meat you're using is tough, marinate for at least 6 hours to tenderize.

Dressings

Why settle for mediocre, store-bought dressings when, in seconds, you can create homemade, wholesome dressings that burst with freshness and flavor? In this section we combine the classics like zesty Bleu Cheese and creamy Thousand Island with exciting new dressing ideas such as bold Basil Mint and Spicy Avocado. And with the Magic Bullet, you control the ingredients so you don't have to worry about salt, preservatives and spices you don't like. Now every salad can be exactly the way you want it.

Basil-Mint Dressing 

You'll savor every bite of this gourmet flavor extravaganza for the taste buds.

1/3 cup olive oil
1 Tbs. of fresh basil
1Tbs. of fresh mint
1 tsp. chives
3 Tbs. red wine vinegar
1/3 tsp. salt
Pinch of pepper

First ... Add all the ingredients to the ***Tall Cup*** and blend with the ***Cross Blade*** until smooth.
Then ... Chill the mixture for about an hour.
Finally ... Toss over salad.

Perfect over sliced tomato, or toss into salad greens.

This dressing gets better with age. Try to prepare it about an hour before serving, or make a double batch and save some in the refrigerator.

Herb Dressing  

This light, flavorful dressing has just the right zing to bring out the best in any salad.

2 stalks celery and leaves
2 small green onions + tops
4 sprigs parsley
1 tsp. paprika

1/4 tsp. dried basil (2 leaves fresh basil)
1/8 tsp. marjoram or rosemary (1 sprig fresh)
1 cup olive oil
2/3 cup lemon juice

First … Add all the ingredients to the ***Blender Attachment*** and blend with the ***Cross Blade*** until smooth.
Then … Chill the mixture for about an hour.
Finally … Toss over salad.

Perfect over any salad, or try dribbling a little over sliced avocado.

This dressing gets better with age. Try to prepare it about an hour before serving time, or make a double batch and save some in the refrigerator.

Bleu Cheese Dressing  

No jar bleu cheese dressing can hold a candle to this fresh and oh-so-creamy blend. You'll want to eat it with a spoon!

1 clove garlic
2 oz. bleu cheese
1 cup mayonnaise
1/4 cup sour cream
2 Tbs. fresh lemon juice
2 Tbs. sugar

First … Add all the ingredients to the ***Tall Cup*** and blend with the ***Cross Blade*** until smooth.
Then … Chill the mixture for about an hour.
Finally … Toss over salad.

Thousand Island Dressing 

This chunky, creamy dressing is an American classic that's not only delicious over any tossed salad, it makes an awesome sandwich spread.

1 cup mayonnaise
2 tsp. horseradish sauce
2 Tbs. vinegar
2 Tbs. sugar
1 thin slice of green bell pepper (about 1/2 oz.)
1 dill pickle
1/2 celery stalk
1 thin slice of onion (about 1/2 oz)
3 Tbs. ketchup
1/2 tsp. paprika
1 hard-boiled egg

First ... Add all the ingredients to the ***Tall Cup*** and **Pulse** 3-4 times with the ***Cross Blade*** until you achieve a slightly chunky consistency.
Then ... Refrigerate until ready to serve.

Perfect over your favorite salad, or it makes a fantastic sandwich spread.

This dressing gets better with time, so chill for as long as you can before serving

Ranch Dressing

This cool and creamy dressing is the perfect topping for any salad, plus it makes an excellent dip for veggie platters.

1 cup mayonnaise
1 garlic clove
1/4 green onion
1 sprig flat-leaf parsley
1/2 tsp. of oregano
2 fresh basil leaves
2 fresh chives
1/4 cup buttermilk
Pinch of salt
Pinch of black pepper

First ... Add all of the ingredients to the ***Blender Attachment*** and **Pulse** with the ***Cross Blade*** until smooth.
Then ... Refrigerate until ready to serve.

Spicy Avocado Dressing  

Tangy and spicy, this Tex-Mex favorite will add just the right amount of kick to your favorite salads. It's also a perfect dressing for grilled vegetables.

2 avocados
2 jalapenos, de-seeded
2/3 cup extra virgin oil
2 garlic cloves
1/4 cup balsamic vinegar
1 Tbs. Dijon mustard
3-5 cherry tomatoes or 1/2 of a regular size tomato
1 1/2 cups water
Salt and pepper to taste

First ... Add all of the ingredients to the ***Blender Attachment*** and **Pulse** with the ***Cross Blade*** until smooth.
Then ... Refrigerate until ready to serve.

Sauces

With the Magic Bullet, it only takes a few seconds to turn a plain chicken breast into succulent, Sweet and Sour Chicken. You don't need knives, a cutting board, whisks or bowls to make delicious sauces, just a Magic Bullet and some basic ingredients you very likely already have in your kitchen. Plus, you control the ingredients! So if you like things spicy, double the jalapeños, or if you're a big fan of garlic, throw in an extra clove. You'll be a "sauce-aholic" in no time!

Cocktail Sauce  

This rich and zesty red sauce will have your taste buds doing a standing ovation.

- 1 cup ketchup
- 2 Tbs. prepared horseradish
- 2 tsp. Worcestershire sauce
- 1 1/2 Tbs. fresh lime juice
- 1 Tbs. chopped cilantro (optional)

First ... Add all the ingredients to the ***Tall Cup*** and blend with the ***Cross Blade*** until smooth.
Then ... Salt and Pepper to taste.

Serve cold with shrimp cocktail and crackers for dipping. Also perfect as dip for fried seafood – shrimp, clams, fish sticks and more.

Bullet Barbecue Sauce  

Here is a rich and tangy Texas twist on ordinary barbeque sauce.

- 1/4 cup olive oil
- 2 Tbs. soy sauce
- 1/4 cup bourbon, sherry, or wine
- 1-2 garlic cloves
- 2-3 peppercorns

First ... Add all the ingredients to the ***Tall Cup*** and blend with the ***Cross Blade*** until smooth.
Then ... Salt and Pepper to taste.

This sauce is perfect as a dip for chicken and beef, or as a basting sauce while barbequing.

Tartar Sauce

This perfect blend of creamy and tangy creates a sauce to remember!

1 cup mayo
1/2 boiler onion (or a 1/4 inch thick slice of a regular-sized onion)
1 Tbs. lemon juice
2 sprigs of dill
1-2 gherkins or dill pickles (or 3 Tbs. pickle relish)

First ... Add all the ingredients to the ***Tall Cup*** and blend with the ***Cross Blade*** until smooth.
Then ... Salt and Pepper to taste.

Tartar Sauce is a perfect dipping sauce with fried fish, or as a spread on fish sandwiches.

5-Second Mock Hollandaise Sauce

It can't be brunch without eggs benedict. Now you can whip up a fresh batch of this safe (no raw egg) Hollandaise in seconds. Delish!

1/4 cup butter or margarine
Juice of 1/2 lemon
1 1/4 cups mayonnaise

First ... Melt the butter in the ***Tall Cup*** by microwaving for 1 minute.
Then ... Add the lemon and mayonnaise and blend with the ***Cross Blade*** until smooth.
Serve immediately.

Swedish Sauce

Like a massage for your taste buds – this light and creamy white sauce is just perfect over meatballs, slices of meatloaf, or chicken.

4 oz. brown gravy (jarred)
2-3 Tbs. sour cream
2-3 sprigs of fresh dill

First … Add the ingredients to the ***Short Cup*** and blend with the ***Cross Blade*** for 2-3 seconds.
Then … Remove the ***Cross Blade*** and microwave on high for 2 - 3 minutes (until thoroughly heated).
Finally … Pour over the top of your cooked meatballs and serve immediately.

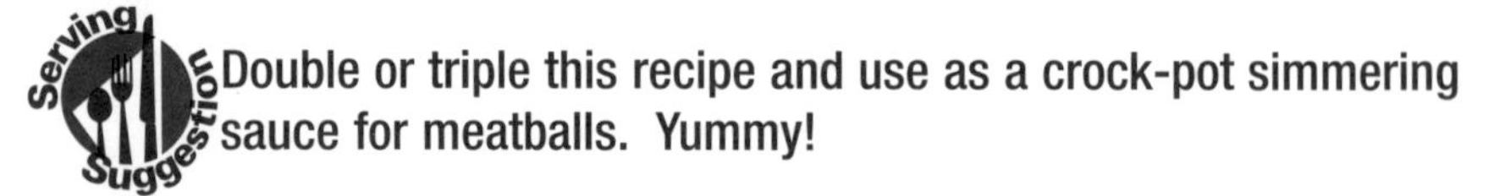

Double or triple this recipe and use as a crock-pot simmering sauce for meatballs. Yummy!

Sweet and Sour Sauce 

Sweet and tangy, snappy and refreshing – pour this "Chinese Food" inspired sauce over chicken, ham, or sliced meatloaf. It's a sauce you'll surely be raving about.

1/2 cup packed brown sugar
1 - 12 or 14oz. can pineapple chunks
1/3 cup vinegar
1 Tbs. soy sauce
1 small pepper (de-seeded and quartered)

First … Add the ingredients to the ***Blender Attachment*** and **Pulse** with the ***Cross Blade*** 5-6 times until the ingredients are mixed, but still a little chunky.

Then … Remove the ***Cross Blade*** and microwave on high for 2-3 minutes or until thoroughly heated.
Finally … Pour over the top of your entree.

Serving Suggestion: Double or triple this recipe and use as a crock-pot simmering sauce for meatballs.

4-Second Sour Cream-Horseradish Sauce

You know that cool and zesty sauce that always comes with Prime Rib? Now you can make it in 4 seconds with your Magic Bullet. It's delicious with any beef, ham, or pork dish, and unbelievably divine when poured over a baked potato.

- 1 cup sour cream
- 2 Tbs. cider vinegar
- 2 Tbs. prepared horseradish sauce
- 1/2 boiler onion, or one thin slice of a regular-sized onion
- 1 sprig of fresh dill

First … Add all the ingredients to the ***Tall Cup*** and blend with the ***Cross Blade*** until smooth.
Then … Chill and serve.

Serving Suggestion: Also try this savory sauce on Roast Beef sandwiches.

6-Second Savory Simmer Sauce

Not sure what to cook for dinner? Try this effortless, fat-free, garlic-tomato simmer sauce and watch your beef, chicken or fish transform from "Whatever" to "Whapow!"

8-10 cherry tomatoes or one regular-sized tomato
(about a 1/4 cup)
2-3 cloves garlic
1/4 cup red wine

First … Add 1 tablespoon of olive oil to a non-stick frying pan over medium-high heat and brown chicken, beef, or pork, heating each piece of meat for about 2 minutes on each side.
Then … Add all of the ingredients to the ***Tall Cup*** and **Pulse** with the ***Cross Blade*** 2-3 times, until you have a slightly chunky texture.
Next … Reduce heat to low, pour the simmer sauce over the meat, and place a lid on the frying pan.
Then … Flip the meat every few minutes, covering it with sauce.
Finally … Simmer the meat until done, about 7-12 minutes depending on the cut. Serve immediately.

Notes: You can use frozen chicken breasts! Following the same recipe, simply brown the chicken for 4-5 minutes on each side, checking every few minutes to keep from scorching. Simmer for about 15 minutes, using a meat thermometer to make sure it's done.

When simmering the meat, scoop spoonfuls of sauce over it to get the most flavor.

Magical Mango Chutney 

Absolutely divine! A simple, tangy, yet fruity topping for meats that will make you look like a culinary wizard. Just add a dollop to magically transform your entrée. Abracadabra!

- 2 mangoes, peeled and seeded
- 1/4 oz. fresh ginger
- 1/4 Spanish onion
- 1 Tbs. rice wine vinegar
- 2 Tbs. sugar
- 1 Tbs. cornstarch
- 2 Tbs. water

First ... Combine the cornstarch and water in the ***Tall Cup*** and **Pulse** with the ***Cross Blade*** 3-4 times.
Then ... Add the remaining ingredients and Pulse until blended, but still slightly chunky.
Next ... Twist off the ***Cross Blade*** and twist on a ***Steamer Top***. Microwave it on medium-high heat for about 1-2 minutes, or until heated thoroughly.
Serve hot, or chill and serve cold.

Chimichurri Sauce

This classic sauce from Argentina is a superb combination of zesty herbs and spices, steeped olive oil and garlic; a fantastic sauce for grilling or dipping. Enjoy!

1 to 15 cloves garlic
1/2 or more red jalapenos (stemmed and seeded)
1/8 cup fresh oregano leaves
1/2 cup fresh parsley leaves
1/8 cup red wine vinegar
1/4 cup olive oil
Pinch of salt

First ... Add all ingredients into the ***Tall Cup*** and **Pulse** with the ***Cross Blade*** until smooth.
Then ... Use immediately or refrigerate until ready to use.

Use as a basting sauce for shrimp, beef, chicken or pork, and/or serve as a sauce on the side of just about any meat or main dish.

Side Dishes

A meal is not a meal without a tasty side dish to finish it off. With the Magic Bullet, you can whip up delicious sides like creamy, cheesy Twice-Baked Potatoes, or spicy Sesame Noodles in just seconds. And these delectable morsels clean up in seconds too!

Twice-Baked Potatoes

These creamy, crunchy, cheesy 'taters are the Holy Grail of comfort food. Nothing so easy has ever tasted so good. The whole family will be begging for these super spuds.

2 russet potatoes
1 scallion
1 oz. cheddar cheese
1 piece of bacon
Splash of milk
1 Tbs. of butter
Pepper

First ... Bake 2 regular-sized russet potatoes at 350 degrees until tender (leave the oven on 350 degrees).
Then ... Cut the potatoes in half and gently scoop out the potato flesh – being careful to keep the skin in one piece (you want it to be like a cup).
Next ... Add the potato and all other ingredients to the ***Tall Cup*** and **Pulse** with the ***Cross Blade*** until the ingredients are mixed together but still textured. (Add more milk if the denseness of the ingredients makes the blending process difficult.)
Then ... Refill the potato skins with the potato mixture.
Finally ... Sprinkle the top of each potato with pepper, place the 4 halves on a baking sheet and return to the oven for 15-20 minutes (unit top is golden brown and cheese is melted).
Serve immediately.

Twice-Baked Potatoes are very versatile, so feel free to play with the ingredients. Tasty add-ins include: broccoli, ham, bleu cheese, red peppers, and spinach. Be creative!

Sesame Noodles  

This is a wonderful twist on the everyday pasta salad. Served hot, these noodles are a scrumptious side to chicken, beef, or fish. Served cold, this zesty dish is just perfect for lunches, potlucks and picnics.

- 1/4 cup soy sauce
- 1/4 cup rice-wine vinegar
- 6 Tbs. cold water
- 1 Tbs. sugar
- 1/2 tsp. salt
- 2 tsp. fresh ginger
- 2 cloves garlic
- 6 Tbs. smooth peanut butter (room temp)
- 3 Tbs. Asian sesame oil
- 1 tsp. hot chili oil
- 12 oz. dried, cooked linguine (al dente)

First … Add all ingredients, except for peanut butter and linguine, and blend with the ***Cross Blade*** until smooth.
Then … Add the peanut butter and blend until smooth.
Next … Toss the sauce over the cooked linguine.
Finally … Chill for an hour and serve.
Or … To serve hot, simply heat the sauce for a minute or two in the microwave, and toss over the warm noodles. (Every microwave is different, monitor it while heating.)

Notes

Makes 6-8 servings.

For a nice finished look, sprinkle a few whole sesame seeds over the top of the noodles.

Potato Pancakes (Latkes) 

Don't throw away your leftover mashed potatoes! These crunchy on the outside, creamy on the inside, potato pancakes will quickly become a breakfast, lunch and dinner tradition in your home.

1 egg
1 cup mashed potato
Splash or 2 of milk
2 scallions (cut off roots and stems)

For frying: 2 Tbs. of olive oil

First ... add the ingredients, in the order they appear, to the ***Blender Attachment***, and **Pulse** with the ***Cross Blade*** until all the ingredients are mixed together but still textured.
Then ... On medium-high, heat 2-3 tablespoons of olive oil in a large frying pan (the pan's surface should have a thin layer of oil).
Next ... Drop the potato mixture by rounded tablespoonfuls into the pan and flatten with a spatula.
Finally ... Fry pancakes until crispy and golden on both sides. Add oil between batches as needed.

Serve with sour cream or applesauce for dipping.

Fried Rice  

Turn your leftover rice into a festive Chinese meal in seconds. This healthy, tasty, simple to make dish is sure to become a household favorite. You may never order take out again!

1/4 cup cooked chicken (or beef)
2 celery stalks
1-2 cloves garlic
3 Tbs. soy sauce
1 cup white or brown rice

First ... Remove most of the celery strings. Crack the celery almost in half and pull the stalks away from the string, breaking them to fit into the ***Tall Cup***.
Then ... Add the chicken, garlic and soy sauce to the celery in the ***Tall Cup*** and **Pulse** with the ***Cross Blade*** until blended but still chunky.
Next ... Place the rice in a slightly greased frying pan and add the chicken mixture to the top.
Finally ... Heat up the rice mixture until hot, and serve immediately.

Serving Suggestion: For a nice and flavorful touch, sprinkle the top of the rice with bamboo shoots, or minced peanuts (use the ***Short Cup*** and the ***Flat Blade*** for mincing).

For a delicious vegetarian dish, simply omit the chicken or beef, and substitute with your favorite frozen or fresh vegetables. Some to try: peas, carrots, broccoli, or zucchini.

Dinners

The question "What's for dinner?" is no longer cause for cringing because, with these Magic Bullet recipes, making dinner is so quick and easy, everyone can have their favorite dish in no time. Now flavorful dishes including delectable Pasta Primavera, Hearty Meatloaf and zesty Sesame Scallops can be prepared in seconds and served to smiling faces that will never know just how easy dinner was to create.

Instant Alla Checca (Tomato/Basil Sauce)

Fresh, simple, and magnificent, this traditional Italian sauce is chock-full of fresh tomato and basil flavor.

10-12 cherry tomatoes or 1-1 1/2 regular sized tomatoes (about a cup)
1/4 cup olive oil
2 cloves garlic
4-6 sprigs of basil
Salt and pepper to taste
Splash of red wine (optional)

First ... Add all ingredients in the order they are listed to the ***Tall Cup*** and twist on the ***Cross Blade***.
Then ... Gently **Pulse** the mixture 5-7 times, making certain not to over-blend. To maintain a chunky consistency, quickly **Pulse** and pause to let the ingredients settle, then repeat that action until you get a slightly chunky consistency.
Next ... Twist off the ***Cross Blade***, replace with the ***Steamer Top***, and place the cup in microwave. Cook the mixture on high for 2 to 3 minutes, or until the sauce is heated thoroughly.
Finally ... Stir and serve over hot pasta.

This recipe makes 1 generous serving of sauce. Double or triple the ingredients and use the ***Blender Attachment*** to make more servings.

Serving Suggestion

Add a little fresh ground parmesan cheese to the top of your piping hot pasta dish! Just add a chunk of parmesan to the ***Short Cup*** and twist on the ***Cross Blade***. Chop until the consistency is a coarse powder. Sprinkle over the top and enjoy!

Mediterranean Pasta Sauce 

This is a very interesting, flavorful twist on traditional pasta sauce. Try it once, and you'll be hooked!

- 1 8 oz. can whole tomatoes (2 regular-sized tomatoes)
- 4 chunks (drained) roasted red pepper (from jar)
- 1/2 jar (3 oz.) marinated artichoke hearts, drained
- 3 cloves garlic
- 1 tsp. cinnamon
- 1/4 small onion (1 boiler onion)
- 1/2 tsp. dried oregano
- 1/2 tsp. dried basil

First ... Blend all the ingredients in the ***Tall Cup*** with the ***Cross Blade*** until you achieve a smooth, but slightly textured consistency.
Then ... Heat the sauce in the microwave for about 3 minutes, or until hot.
Finally ... Pour over hot pasta and serve.

Pronto Primavera  

This pasta dish is a perfect light meal. The flavorful, wispy sauce adds just the right zing to the piping hot vegetables without weighing them down. This is a meal that is perfect for unexpected guests. With these basic ingredients, and a few seconds to spare, you can whip up a tasty, Italian classic that will have your guests licking their plates!

- 2 Tbs. olive oil
- 2/3 cup vegetable (or chicken) broth
- Chunk of Parmesan

Dinners

1-2 cloves garlic
splash of white wine (optional)
1 cup of your favorite steamed vegetables
Linguini noodles

First ... Add all ingredients, except the vegetables and pasta, in to the ***Tall Cup***, twist on the ***Cross Blade*** and **Pulse** 5-7 times.
Then ... Twist off the ***Cross Blade***, add your favorite veggies (broccoli, carrots, mushrooms, peppers, etc.) then twist on the ***Steamer Top*** and place the cup in the microwave.
Next ... Cook sauce on high for 4 to 6 minutes, or until the vegetables are tender.
Finally ... Stir and serve over hot pasta.

This recipe makes one generous serving of sauce

Serving Suggestion: Add a little fresh ground parmesan cheese to the top of your piping hot pasta dish! Just add a chunk of parmesan to the ***Short Cup*** and twist on the ***Cross Blade***. Chop until the consistency is a coarse powder. Sprinkle over the top and enjoy!

Tips: ***Use Frozen Italian Vegetables*** If you want Super Easy Pasta Primavera, after mixing the sauce, add frozen Italian veggies (from the freezer section of your grocery store) to the ***Tall Cup*** and microwave for about 2-3 minutes, or until the vegetables are cooked. Then, simply pour over pasta.

Mighty Quick Mini Meatloaf   

This light, fluffy, flavorful meatloaf is a tasty treat for one and, all and couldn't be easier to make. Picture this: you walk in the door from work, you throw the ingredients in the Magic Bullet and in seconds you're putting your dinner in the oven. You put your feet up, and half an hour later your delicious, piping hot, homemade meatloaf is ready.

1 egg
1/2 lb. ground beef (or turkey)
1/3 cup bread crumbs
1/3 cup onion
1 tsp. parsley flakes
Pinch of black pepper
Splash of chicken stock

First … Add ingredients in the order they are listed to the ***Tall Cup*** and **Pulse** with the ***Cross Blade*** until blended but still a little textured.
Then … Pour into a greased mini loaf pan and bake for 30-40 minutes at 350 degrees or until done.

Notes: This recipe is the perfect size to cook in a mini-loaf pan. For a full-sized meatloaf, double the ingredients and use the ***Blender Attachment*** for mixing. For best blender results, chop onions first, add the rest of the ingredients, and mix.

Serving Suggestion: Top with either the Swedish Sauce (page 62) or the Sweet and Sour Sauce (page 62-63).

Tips: ***Mighty Quick Meatballs*** Instead of adding to a loaf pan, roll the ingredients into meatballs and bake for 30 minutes at 350 degrees. From sports night to toddler birthday parties, both the Swedish (page 62) and Sweet and Sour Meatballs (page 62-63) are a sure crowd pleaser.

Crock-Pot Meatballs Instead of baking, add meatballs to the crock-pot with either the Swedish or Sweet and Sour Sauce. Cook meatballs on low for 4-5 hours, high for 2 hours, or until the meat is cooked.

No breadcrumbs No worries. Make your own by placing a piece of bread, a little parmesan and some Italian spices in the ***Short Cup***, and **Pulse** a few times (even stale bread works!). Or throw in a few croutons instead.

Sesame Sea Scallops

Now you see the scallops, now you don't. Tired of burgers and hot dogs? Try this simple, fantastic tasting, spicy scallop kabob recipe at your next barbeque. Your guests will be licking their plates and begging for the recipe!

- 1 Tbs. sesame oil
- 2 Tbs. white wine
- 1/4 cup soy sauce
- 1-2 cloves garlic
- 2 tsp. fresh ginger (or 1/8 tsp. ground ginger)
- Dash garlic salt
- Dash pepper
- 1 lb. large sea scallops
- 1 Tbs. sesame seeds

First … Add all the ingredients, except for the scallops and sesame seeds, into the ***Short Cup*** and blend with the ***Cross Blade*** until smooth.
Then … Pour the mixture over the scallops and marinate in the refrigerator for 30 minutes to 1 hour.
Next … Thread the scallops onto skewers.
Then … Place on the grill and cook for 5 minutes or until done. Turn halfway through cooking time.
Finally … Sprinkle with sesame seeds and serve immediately.

Add your favorite veggie chunks to the skewers for a healthy side dish.

Use sea scallops rather than smaller bay scallops, which are very hard to thread onto the skewers.

Desserts

Homemade desserts have never been easier. With the Magic Bullet, you can whip up tangy, creamy Key Lime Pie, a fancy, fruity, delicious Fruit Tart and a Chocolate Cream Pie to die for, all in just seconds and all with such ease, you'll never step foot in a bakery again. Enjoy!

10-Second Tiramisu 

This light and fluffy pastry crust, drizzled with espresso is topped with creamy, chocolaty goodness. It's an Italian celebration for the mouth!

- 2/3 cup of powdered sugar
- 1 8oz. package of cream cheese (room temperature)
- 1 cup of plain yogurt
- 2 cups of whipped cream
- 1/2 cup sweetened espresso (or strong coffee)
- 18 ladyfingers (pastry-like little cakes)

First ... Add the powdered sugar, cream cheese, yogurt and 1 cup of whipped cream to the ***Blender Attachment*** and blend with the ***Cross Blade*** until smooth.
Then ... Split the lady fingers and spread the bottom halves out in an 8" baking dish. Drizzle them with 1/2 the coffee.
Next ... Spread 1/2 of the yogurt mixture on top, then repeat with the next layer of lady fingers and remaining yogurt mixture.
Finally ... Top with the remaining whipped cream, sprinkle the top with cocoa powder, and chill for at least 2 hours before serving.

Chocolate Cream Pie   

Never before has something this easy tasted so unbelievably good. From start to serve, you can make this utterly divine dessert in just 10 seconds and with only one cup to clean. It really is magic!

- 8 oz. whipping cream
- 1/4 cup chocolate syrup
- 1 graham cracker crust

First ... Add whipping cream and chocolate syrup to the ***Tall Cup*** and whip with the ***Flat Blade*** until creamy.

Then … Pour into graham cracker crust, spread to fill pie shell and serve.

Notes: You can actually hear when the whipping process is complete. The sound of the blade changes from a heavy whirring to a light whirring.

Serving Suggestion: Grind up a small chocolate bar with the ***Cross Blade*** and sprinkle over the top of the pie, or whip up some whipped cream and add a dollop to each slice of pie, then sprinkle with a little ground chocolate. You can also sprinkle with a little cocoa powder.

Crazy Quick Carrot Cake

This moist, delicious classic cake is simply bursting with fresh flavor, and never before have you experienced a lighter, fluffier glaze. It's so easy, you'll be making carrot cakes all the time!

- 1/2 pkg. yellow cake mix
- 2 eggs
- 2 Tbs. oil
- 1/4 cup water
- 2 Tbs. packed brown sugar
- 1 tsp. cinnamon
- 1 cup baby carrots
- 1/4 cup raisins
- 1/4 cup chopped nuts

First … Preheat oven to 350 degrees.
Then … Add the baby carrots to the ***Tall Cup*** and **Pulse** with the ***Cross Blade*** until very small but still chunky.

Now ... Add all ingredients, except for the raisins and nuts, with the carrots to the ***Blender Attachment***, and blend with the ***Cross Blade*** until smooth.
Next ... Add the raisins and nuts to the mixture and **Pulse** 3 or 4 times.
Then ... Pour into a 13 x 9-inch baking pan (or two 8-inch pans) and bake for 30-40 minutes.
While it's cooking ... Prepare glaze recipe (below) and refrigerate.
Next ... Remove cake from oven and let cool for 15 minutes.
Finally ... Frost the cake with the glaze and serve.

Cake Glaze (Basic Cake Frosting) 

1/2 cup powdered sugar
1 1/2 oz. cream cheese
2 Tbs. milk
1 tsp. vanilla

First ... Add all the ingredients to the ***Tall Cup*** and blend with the ***Flat Blade*** until smooth.
Then ... Refrigerate until the carrot cake is ready.

10-Second Fresh Fruit Tart 

At last, a creamy, delicious fruity dessert you can make in seconds. You've never had a lighter, fluffier fruit tart!

8 oz. cream cheese, softened
1 Tbs. orange zest (peel)
2 Tbs. orange juice
1/2 cup confectioner's sugar
1 baked 9-inch refrigerator pie shell (or 6 mini tart shells)
2 cups fresh fruit, such as fresh whole blackberries or raspberries

First ... Blend the cheese, zest, juice, and sugar together in the ***Tall Cup*** with the ***Cross Blade*** until fluffy.
Then ... Fill pie crust or tart shells with cheese mixture and chill thoroughly.
Finally ... Top with slices of preferred fruit.

Add 1 Tbs. lemon juice to fruit such as peaches or nectarines to prevent discoloration. Sprinkle sugar generously over fruit.

Dirt Cake   

This chocolate mousse-like cake recipe is perfect for kids' birthday parties. For girls, it's a flower cake; simply add a lovely plastic flower to the top. For boys, it's a dirt cake; load it up with gummy bugs and coconut grass. This creamy, delicious cake will provide endless amounts of smiles.

1 package Oreo™ cookies
1/2 gallon of heavy cream
2 cups Hershey™ chocolate syrup
2 package of gummy worms
1 package of coconut
Green food coloring
Plastic flowers or gummy bugs
1 package of mini candy bars
8 small terra cotta pots or 8 clear plastic cups

First ... Fill the ***Tall Cup*** with as many Oreos as you can fit and blend with the ***Cross Blade*** until smooth. Repeat until all of the Oreos™ are a fine powder, (i.e. "Dirt") and set aside in a sealed plastic container.
Next ... Make a batch of Chocolate

Mousse by adding 24 oz. of whipping cream and 1/3 cup of chocolate syrup to the ***Blender Attachment*** and blending with the ***Flat Blade*** until whipped. Refrigerate in a sealed plastic container.
Then … Add 2-3 cups of coconut and 1 Tbs. of green food coloring to a sealed plastic container (or use a ***Tall Cup*** with a ***Stay-Fresh Re-sealable Lid***). Mix the coconut and green dye until it looks grassy-green (add more dye if necessary) and set aside in the container.
Next … Use either one large terra cotta flower pot, or 6-8 small pots. Start by blocking the hole in the bottom with a piece of foil, then add a layer of Oreo "dirt", a thick layer of chocolate mousse (add gummy worms into mousse), and another layer of Oreo dirt.
Finally … Finish off the cake(s) by decorating with gummy worms, bugs, plastic flowers and coconut grass.

Couldn't Be Easier Key Lime Pie

This light and tasty pie is simply divine. The mouth-watering contrast of creamy and tangy guarantees a marvelous dessert experience worthy of praise.

1 9-inch pie shell, baked
1 14 oz. can sweetened condensed milk
1/2 cup Key lime or regular lime juice (about the juice of 4 limes)
A ***Short Cup*** of heavy cream
1 Tbs. finely grated lime peel

First … Use the ***Short Cup*** and ***Cross Blade*** to grate slices of lime peel and set aside.
Then … Fill the ***Short Cup*** just about to the top with heavy cream and mix with the ***Flat Blade*** until a whipped cream consistency is achieved (you'll hear when it's ready).
Next … Add the condensed milk, lime juice, grated lime peel and half of the whipped cream to the ***Tall Cup*** and blend with the ***Cross***

Blade until smooth.
Finally ... Pour the contents of the ***Tall Cup*** into the pie shell, the gently stir in the remaining whipped cream.
Then ... Chill for at least one hour before serving.

7-Second Snow Cones  

Your kids will love these so much, they will never believe they're healthy. Perfect summertime treats for children and adults.

1 cups ice
1/4 cup fruit juice or snow cone flavoring

First ... Fill the ***Tall Cup*** with ice and grind with the ***Cross Blade*** until you achieve a slush-like consistency.
Then ... Pour fruit juice or snow cone flavoring on the top and serve.

Tips We found that scooping the slushy ice as it accumulates near the blade gave us the best consistency.
Snow cone flavoring Most grocery stores sell snow cone flavoring. It comes in the classic cherry, orange and grape flavors.

Easy As Pumpkin Pie 

This creamy, spicy, delectable pie is so very delicious, your friends and family won't believe how effortless it was. Volunteer to bring it to your next holiday party, and you'll be the talk of the town.

1 ready-made 9-inch pie crust (graham or regular flavor)
3/4 cup light brown sugar
1/2 tsp. salt
1 tsp. cinnamon
1/2 tsp. ground ginger
1/4 tsp. ground cloves
2 eggs
1 15 oz. can solid pack pumpkin
1 12 oz. can evaporated milk

First ... Preheat the oven to 350 degrees.
Then ... Place all ingredients, except the pie crust, into the ***Blender Attachment***.
Next ... Blend with the ***Cross Blade*** until smooth.
Finally ... Pour the pumpkin mixture into the pie shell and bake for 45 minutes or until firm.

Add a dollop of fresh whipped cream to the top of each pie slice and sprinkle with cinnamon, nutmeg or cocoa powder.

Quick Breads and Biscuits

You asked for it, you got it – a Quick Breads and Biscuits section. These simple to make, awesome to eat recipes range from moist, delicious Fiesta Corn Bread to sweet and tasty Cinnamon Raisin Biscuits. So forget the spoons, bowls, apron and rolling pins – now you can prepare scrumptious baked goods, practically mess free, and in less time than it takes to heat the oven.

Chocolate Bread 

Chocolate bread, what more needs to be said? Fresh-from-the-oven, warm bread with melted bits of chocolate is definitely not one to miss!

- 1/3 cup firmly packed brown sugar
- 1/4 cup Butter, melted
- 1/2 cup semi-sweet chocolate chips
- 1 large egg
- 1 tsp. vanilla extract
- 1 1/4 cups all-purpose flour
- 3/4 cup applesauce
- 1/2 tsp. baking powder
- 1/2 tsp. baking soda

First ... Preheat the oven to 350 degrees.
Then ... Combine all the ingredients in the ***Blender Attachment***.
Next ... **Pulse** with the ***Cross Blade*** until the batter is blended. (If you want bigger chunks of melted chocolate in your bread, **Pulse** only 3 or 4 times, then use a spoon to stir the batter once or twice.)
Then ... Pour the batter into a greased loaf pan.
Finally ... Bake for 35-42 minutes.

Pumpkin Bread 

This zesty, cake-like bread will have your taste buds standing at attention. Perfect for breakfast, or as a dessert, this is sure to become a new family favorite.

- 1 1/8 cup flour
- 1/4 tsp. cinnamon
- 1 tsp baking powder
- 1/2 tsp. salt

1/8 tsp. ground ginger
Pinch of nutmeg
Pinch of allspice
1 egg
1 cup sugar
1 cup pumpkin purée (8 oz. can)
1/4 cup vegetable oil

First … Preheat the oven to 350 degrees.
Next … Combine all the ingredients in the ***Blender Attachment*** and **Pulse** with the ***Cross Blade*** until smooth.
Then … Spoon mixture into a greased and floured 9x5x2-inch loaf pan and bake at 350 degrees for about 55 minutes.

Fabulously Fast Fiesta Corn Bread

Are you ready for a palate party? This zesty, ultra-moist twist on everyday cornbread is sure to become a dinner staple. Muy bueno!

1 8 1/2 oz. package of corn muffin mix
1 egg
1/3 cup milk
1/2 cup cream-style corn
1/2 (or more to taste) jalapeño pepper
1/4 cup Sour Cream
1/4 of a green bell pepper
1 oz. chunk cheddar cheese
(or 1/4 cup shredded)

First … Preheat the oven to 400 degrees
Then … Add the jalapeño and cheddar cheese to the ***Blender Attachment*** and **Pulse** using the

Cross Blade a few times until minced.
Next ... Add the remaining ingredients and **Pulse** until the batter is blended.
Finally ... Pour the batter into a greased loaf pan and bake for 20-25 minutes.

Cheese-Garlic Biscuits

Cheese and garlic add a little "big city" pizzazz to the classic biscuit. So delicious, you'll have to hide them from yourself!

- 2-3 oz. Cheddar cheese (chunk, or shredded)
- 2 cups Original Bisquick
- 2/3 cup milk
- 2 Tbs. butter (or margarine)
- 1 clove of garlic (1/8 tsp. garlic powder)

First ... Preheat oven to 450 degrees.
Then ... Twist the ***Cross Blade*** on to the ***Blender Attachment*** and add the Bisquick milk, and cheese. If using a chunk of cheese, cut it into thirds and add it to the ***Blender Attachment*** first. **Pulse** a few times until it's shredded, then add the other ingredients.
Next ... Place the ***Blender Attachment*** on the ***Power Base*** and mix until the ingredients are blended. (Be careful not to run your Magic Bullet too long. Blend for less than a minute and pause for a few seconds before resuming.)
Then ... Sprinkle a flat surface (plate or counter top) with Bisquick, remove the dough from the ***Blender Attachment*** and roll it out until it's a 1/2-inch thick.
Next ... Cut the dough into 2 1/2-inch circles and place on an ungreased cookie sheet.
When the biscuits are about done ... Add the butter, or margarine, and garlic to the ***Short Cup*** and heat in the microwave until melted.
Then ... Twist on the ***Cross Blade*** and **Pulse** the butter mixture a

few times until the garlic is minced.
Finally ... Brush the butter mixture over the warm biscuits.

8-Second Cinnamon-Raisin Biscuits 

These delicious sweet and fruity biscuits are simply perfect with a cup of coffee. Or, throw one in your kid's lunchbox for a special snack-time treat that screams "made with love".

2 cups Bisquick™
1/2 cup milk
1/3 cup granulated sugar
1/3 cup raisins
1 tsp. cinnamon

First ... Preheat oven to 450 degrees.
Then ... Twist the ***Cross Blade*** on to the ***Blender Attachment*** and add all the ingredients inside.
Next ... Place the ***Blender Attachment*** on the ***Power Base*** and mix until the ingredients are blended. (Be careful not to run your Magic Bullet too long. Blend for less than a minute and pause for a few seconds before resuming.)
Then ... Sprinkle a flat surface (plate or counter top) with Bisquick then remove the dough from the ***Blender Attachment*** and roll it out until it's a 1/2-inch thick.
Next ... Cut the dough into 1 1/2-inch circles and place on an ungreased cookie sheet.
Finally ... Bake the biscuit for 8 to 10 minutes, or until golden brown.

Positively Perfect Parmesan-Herb Biscuits

Put a little kick in your biscuit. This cheesy, herb-laden blend is a flavor extravaganza. Warm and chewy with a zesty zing — you simply can't go wrong!

- 2 cups Bisquick™
- 2/3 cup milk
- 1/2 tsp. chopped fresh parsley
- 2 Tbs. grated Parmesan cheese
- 1 Tbs. granulated sugar
- 1/2 tsp. dried sage leaves

Topping
1 Tbs. butter or margarine, melted
1 Tbs. grated Parmesan cheese

First … Preheat oven to 450 degrees.
Then … Twist the ***Cross Blade*** on to the ***Blender Attachment*** and add the Bisquick, milk, cheese and herbs. If using a chunk of cheese, add it to the ***Blender Attachment*** first and **Pulse** a few times until shredded, then add the other ingredients.
Next … Place the ***Blender Attachment*** on the ***Power Base*** and mix until the ingredients are blended. (Be careful not to run your Magic Bullet too long. Blend for less than a minute and pause for a few seconds before resuming.)
Then … Sprinkle a flat surface (plate or counter top) with Bisquick ™ then remove the dough from the ***Blender Attachment*** and roll it out until it's a 1/2-inch thick. Cut into 2 1/2-inch circles.
Next … Place on an ungreased cookie sheet. Bake for 8 to 10 minutes, or until golden brown.
When the biscuits are almost done … Add the butter, or margarine, and Parmesan cheese to the ***Short Cup*** and heat in the microwave until melted.
Then … Twist on the ***Cross Blad***e and **Pulse** the butter mixture a few times until the garlic is minced.
Finally … Brush the butter mixture over the warm biscuits.

Baby Food

Now you can make 100% pure and natural, homemade baby food in just seconds, and for a fraction of the price of jarred baby food. Finally, you will know exactly what your baby is eating. Create your own special blends, or use organic fruits and vegetables. It's all up to you. No muss, no fuss!

Sweet Potato-Turkey   

1 cup raw sweet potato
1 -2 oz. cooked turkey
Splash of water

First ... Steam chunks of sweet potato and water in the ***Short Cup*** until tender.
Next ... Twist on ***Cross Blade*** and blend until smooth.
Finally ... Let cool and serve.

Chicken and Peas   

1-2 oz. cooked chicken
2 Tbs. cooked peas
1/4 cup rice, cooked

First ... Add left over chicken, peas, rice and a splash of water (or chicken broth) to the ***Short Cup***.
Then ... Twist on ***Cross Blade*** and blend until smooth.
Finally ... Heat the ***Short Cup*** for 30 seconds in the microwave, checking the temperature before serving.

Pasta Puree   

Now you're tot can say, "I'll have what she's having". There's no need to make another meal, or to eat from a jar when in a few seconds, you can turn you're spaghetti and meatballs into a yummy baby food.

Ready to serve pasta
1 Tbs. water

First … Add cooked pasta and a splash of water (or chicken broth) to the ***Short Cup***.
Then … Twist on ***Cross Blade*** and blend until smooth.
Finally … Heat if necessary.

Applesauce    

1 small apple (cored)
3 Tbs. water

First … Steam chunks of apple and water in the ***Short Cup*** until tender.
Next … Twist on ***Cross Blade*** and blend until smooth.
Then … Let cool and serve.

Pear Puree

1 small pear (cored)
3 Tbs. water

Firs t ... Steam chunks of pear and water in the ***Short Cup*** with the ***Steamer Top*** on until tender.
And ... Strain off any excess water (keep the ***Steamer Top*** on and just flip the cup to strain).
Next ... Remove the ***Steamer Top***, twist on ***Cross Blade*** and blend until smooth.
Then ... Let cool and serve.

Smoothies and Fat Loss Protein Shakes

T The Magic Bullet is absolutely perfect for making frosty, delicious, satisfying Smoothies, because with the one-of-a-kind *Party Mugs*, you can blend and drink your smoothie out of the same cup! Plus, just add a scoop of protein powder to any one of these recipes and you've got yourself a tasty, couldn't-be-easier, Meal Replacement drink that is hands down the best weight loss drink you've ever tasted. Whether you're on the 6 Week Body Makeover, Atkins, or just looking for a healthy, delicious meal that can be made in seconds, this Smoothie section has got you covered!

It's easy to boost up any one of these smoothie recipes by adding healthy herbs, vitamins and minerals. Whether you're into wheat grass, ginko biloba, or acidopholus, you can slip these into a smoothie and get the health benefits without having to down a bunch of pills or powders. And parents, this is a great way to keep your children healthy without objections.

Strawberry-Pineapple Smoothie

A tropical extravaganza for the taste buds! Fruity, frosty, fantastic!

1 medium banana
1/2 cup pineapple juice
A handful of strawberries
1/4 cup orange juice
1 Tbs. of coconut cream
Ice

First ... Add all ingredients to the ***Tall Cup*** or ***Party Mug*** and twist on the ***Cross Blade***.
Then ... Lock on, mix until smooth, and serve.

6 Week Body Makeover Meal Replacement Drink

The 6-Week Body Makeover, one of America's most popular diets, highly recommends this meal replacement drink. This sweet treat is a perfect meal replacement any day of the week. Creamy and fruity, with just a touch of the tropics, this drink is sure to satisfy your sweet tooth.

1 scoop chocolate protein powder
1 Tbs. Sugar-free coconut syrup
1 Tbs. Sugar-free chocolate syrup

1/2 a banana
1/4 cup of water
Ice

First … Add all ingredients to the ***Tall Cup*** or ***Party Mug*** and twist on the ***Cross Blade***.
Then … Lock on, mix until smooth, and serve.

This recipe is for a drinkable consistency, for a more ice cream-like consistency fill the ***Tall Cup*** 2/3 with ice.

Apple Pie Pre-Workout Smoothie

Now you can power up for the gym in seconds. Just whip up this delectable, thick and creamy smoothie and you'll be ready to go the distance!

1/2 cup cold, cooked oatmeal
1/2 apple, cut in large chunks
1/2 tsp. cinnamon
1 scoop vanilla protein powder
1-2 packets Splenda, depending on how sweet you like your drinks
2/3-1 cup cold water

First … Add the ingredients to the ***Tall Cup*** this order apple chunks, oatmeal, protein powder, cinnamon and Splenda. Pour the water in last.
Then … Twist on the ***Cross Blade*** and blend until smooth.

Low-Carb Caramel Smoothie

For those of you on a low-carb diet, how would you like a rich, creamy caramel smoothie with only one gram of carbs? This quick and easy Atkins-friendly drink is sure to please.

3 ice cubes
1/2 cup of water
2 Tbs. of heavy cream
2 Tbs. of Sugar-free Caramel Syrup

First ... Add all ingredients to the ***Tall Cup*** or ***Party Mug*** and twist on the ***Cross Blade.***
Then ... Lock on, mix until smooth, and serve.

Sugar-free syrups come in many different flavors, so feel free to swap the chocolate syrup with raspberry, hazelnut, or caramel.

Zone-Friendly Pineapple Shake

This is a smooth and creamy sensation that's the perfect morning or afternoon snack. Yummy!

7 oz. Tofu, drained well and cubed (3 blocks protein)
1 cup cubed pineapple (2 blocks carbs)
1 cup low-fat milk (1 block each protein and carb)
3 Macadamia nuts, crushed (3 blocks fat)

First ... Add all ingredients to the ***Tall Cup*** or ***Party Mug*** and twist on the ***Cross Blade***.
Then ... Lock on, mix until smooth, and serve.

Vanilla Cappuccino Protein Drink

How about a morning snack with a kick? This lip-smacking, delicious blended coffee drink is the perfect way to revitalize and nourish at the same time.

- 2 oz. of strong black coffee
- 1 scoop Vanilla protein powder
- 2 packets of Splenda™
- 1 Tbs. Sugar Free chocolate flavored syrup
- 1 cup of ice

First … Add all ingredients to the ***Tall Cup*** or ***Party Mug*** and twist on the ***Cross Blade***.
Then … Lock on, mix until smooth, and serve.

Frosty Fruit Smoothie

Chock full of fruit and fiber, this satisfying and refreshing drink is a taste sensation.

- 1 banana
- 1/2 apple, sliced
- 4-6 frozen peaches
- 2 good splashes of milk
- 1 splash of orange juice
- 1-2 scoops vanilla protein powder (optional)
- Ice

First … Add all ingredients to the ***Tall Cup*** or ***Party Mug*** and twist on the ***Cross Blade***.
Then … Lock on, mix until smooth, and serve.

The Bullet Blizzard

This particular blend of ingredients makes a thick, delicious, creamy smoothie that's so much like ice cream, you may have to eat it with a spoon! You're going to dream about this smoothie at night and wake up early just to throw one back!

1 cup of milk (skim)
7-8 frozen peaches
3-4 ice cubes
1-3 scoops of chocolate protein powder

First … Add all ingredients to the ***Tall Cup*** or ***Party Mug*** and twist on the ***Cross Blade***.
Then … Lock on, mix until smooth, and serve.

The Creamsicle

A modern twist on the old-time favorite! So good, you're going to make this smoothie again and again.

2 scoops vanilla ice cream (or frozen yogurt)
2/3 cup of orange juice
3-4 peeled orange slices
4-6 ice cubes

First … Add all ingredients to the ***Tall Cup*** or ***Party Mug*** and twist on the ***Cross Blade***.
Then … Lock on, mix until smooth, and serve.

Notes: This recipe makes one serving. For more than one serving, just multiply each ingredient by the number of servings you want to make and use the ***Blender Attachment*** for mixing your ingredients.

Juices

Studies show that consuming five or more fruits and vegetables a day reduces the risk of Heart Disease, High Blood Pressure, Diabetes and Cancer. Making fresh juice is a quick and tasty way to meet your daily fruit and vegetable quota. And with the Magic Bullet *Juice Extractor* kit, juicing is so easy there is no reason not to make healthy fruit and vegetable juice cocktails, loaded with vitamins and minerals, every day of the week. The best part of juicing is that you can mask the strong flavors of healthy, but not particularly tasty, vegetables behind delicious fruit flavors like lemon and watermelon. Go ahead and drink your way to good health!

Key reminders about juicing! (See page 29-32 of the Magic Bullet User Guide for detailed Juicing Instructions.)

- **Always turn the *Juice Extractor* on before adding anything into the extractor.**
- **If something gets stuck in the blade, or if the blade stops moving, turn off the power immediately.**
- **Never run the *Juice Extractor* for more than a minute. Pause for a few seconds and start again.**
- **For a pleasant, efficient juicing experience, have your ingredients within arms reach and sized so they will fit into the *Juice Extractor*.**

Fresh Apple Juice

If Johnny Appleseed had this juice recipe, he would have never left his house. It's pure, thirst quenching, apple perfection.

3 apples

First … Cut the apple into quarters and remove seeds.
Next … Add the pieces into the ***Juice Extractor*** and push down with the ***Plunger***.
Then … Pour into a juice glass.

The apple "pulp" that is left in the inside of the ***Juice Extractor*** is the best tasting applesauce we've ever tried!

Mood Lifting Melonade

This smooth, mellow, thirst-quenching drink has just the right amount of lemony tang to turn that frown upside-down.

1/2 peeled lemon
3-4 cups watermelon

First … Prepare the fruit by peeling the lemon and cutting it into wedges, then remove the watermelon rind and cut it into cubes
Next … Add the lemon wedges into the ***Juice Extractor*** and push down with the plunger.
Then … Add the cubes of watermelon into the ***Juice Extractor*** and push down with the ***Plunger***.
Finally … Pour over ice.

Comfort Cocktail

When it's time to relax, put your feet up and let this rich, hearty, natural sleep aid be the gateway to chill time.

10-12 baby carrots
1 handful of parsley
1 stalk celery

First ... Add carrots into the ***Juice Extractor*** and push down with the ***Plunger***.
Next ... Add the parsley and gently push down with the ***Plunger***.
Then ... Add celery and push down with the ***Plunger***.
Finally ... Pour over ice.

Tips The "strings" on celery are bothersome to most people and can make juicing a little more difficult. A great and easy way to remove most of the string is to bend the stalk in half and pull away from the strings.

Clear Complexion Cocktail

Is it breakout city time? This drink is perfect for clearing up blemishes. Your teenagers are going to LOVE this drink!

15-20 baby carrots
1/2 of a green pepper

First ... Cut the pepper in half and then cut the half into thin slices.
Then ... Add the carrots into the ***Juice Extractor*** and push down with the ***Plunger***.
Next ... Add the green pepper slices and push down with the ***Plunger***.
Finally ... Pour over ice.

Cleansing Cocktail

Finally there is a tasty, all natural way to flush the toxins from your body – the perfect hangover drink.

10 - 12 baby carrots
1/2 cucumber (1/3 English cucumber)
1/2 a beet with the greens

First ... Cut the cucumber into strips and cut 1/2 of a beet into small wedges.
Next ... Add the carrots into the ***Juice Extractor*** and push down with the ***Plunger***.
Then ... Add the cucumber strips into the ***Juice Extractor*** and push down with the ***Plunger***.
Now ... Add the beet pieces and the beet greens into the ***Juice Extractor*** and push down with the ***Plunger***.
And ... Serve over ice.

The Tropicana Cocktail

Need a vacation from your daily vocation? Take five with this tropical treat for the taste buds, and you'll be ready to face the world again.

1/4 of a pineapple (peeled and cut into strips)
2 handfuls of green grapes
4-6 strawberries

First ... Cut the pineapple into strips and add the pieces into the ***Juice Extractor***.
Next ... Add the grapes to the ***Juice Extractor*** and push down with the ***Plunger***.
Then ... Add the strawberries to the ***Juice Extractor*** and push down with the ***Plunger***.
And ... Pour into a juice glass.

Magic Bullet Party Ideas

Are you ready to throw a Bullet Bash? These step-by-step party instructions hold your hand through the whole process — every step of the way. From sending out invitations, to shopping lists and party activities, these Party Ideas are the soup-to-nuts way to throw a fabulous party, without all the work.

Whether you choose the Fancy Brunch Party, or the Kid's Birthday Party, simply follow these steps, and you'll be serving your smiling guests gourmet foods and cocktails with the greatest of ease. And the best part is you won't be slaving away in the kitchen. With the Magic Bullet, the party practically throws itself. Have a ball!

The "Sports/Movie Night" Party

This menu was created to make 10 of your friends happy and to put you in your place…right in front of the television screen!

Guests Arrive to:
Super Quick Clam Dip and Sesame Crackers
Lickety Split Cheese Dip and Tortilla Chips
Crock-pot Hot Wings
Frozen Margaritas
Sodas

Main Course:
Pronto Primavera
Garlic Bread

Dessert:
French Roast Coffee
Chocolate Mousse

SHOPPING LIST

Dairy Section

4 oz. cream cheese
8 oz. cheddar (or Velveeta™) cheese
Milk
4 oz. parmesan cheese
Butter
Whipping Cream
Chocolate Syrup

Sauces/Seasonings/Soups Section

Worcestershire sauce
Tabasco™ pepper sauce
Mayonnaise
Vinegar-based barbecue sauce
Salsa (mild, medium or hot)
Vegetable (or chicken) broth
Olive oil

Produce Section

1 bag of boiler onions or 2 regular onions
2 sprigs fresh parsley (no stem)
2 sprigs fresh cilantro
1 jar of peeled, fresh garlic cloves
5 jalapeño peppers
Your favorite vegetables (for the Primavera)

Meats

4 lbs. chicken wings
1 6.5 oz. can minced clams

Beverages Section

Margarita Mix (2 large bottles)
Tequila (1 quart)
Splash of white wine (optional)

French Roast Coffee Beans
Ice

Pasta/Bread Section
2 pkgs. of Linguini noodles
2 large loaves of French bread
Sesame Crackers (or your favorite fancy cracker)
Large bag of Tortilla Chips

Misc.
Aluminum Foil
10 Napkins
10 Dinner Plates
10 Margarita Glasses
Pasta Serving Bowl
Tongs for Hot Wings

FIVE HOURS BEFORE PARTY TIME

Step 1: Prepare the Crock-Pot Hot Wings by following the recipe on page 22. Cook the Wings in a crock-pot for 4 hours, or until done, on the High setting.

ONE HOUR BEFORE PARTY TIME

Step 1: Prepare a batch of Clam Dip, following the recipe on page 13, and chill in the refrigerator.
Step 2: Prepare a batch of Cheese Dip (don't heat yet!) following the recipe on page 14, and chill in the refrigerator.
Step 3: Make a triple batch of Pasta Primavera Sauce in the ***Blender Attachment*** (don't cook the veggies yet) by following the recipe on page 76, and then chill in the refrigerator.
Step 4: Make the garlic bread spread. Microwave 1/4 cup of butter in the ***Short Cup*** until melted, add 2-3 cloves of garlic and a 1-2 oz. chunk of parmesan cheese, and **Pulse** until it's a smooth saucy consistency.
Step 5: Slice the French bread down the middle, spread on the

garlic butter, cut the bread into serving size slices, and wrap the loaves in aluminum foil.

Step 6: Check on the Hot Wings. If they seem done, or really close, turn them down to the Low setting.

Step 7: Add about 2 oz. of Parmesan cheese to the ***Short Cup*** and grate with the ***Cross Blade***. Store it in the refrigerator.

Step 8: Prepare a large batch of Chocolate Mousse by whipping 1 cup of whipping cream and 1/4 cup of chocolate syrup in the ***Tall Cup*** with the ***Flat Blade***. Scoop out the mousse and put it into pudding cups. Then make some whipped cream (see instructions page 24 of the 10 Second Recipes book) and add a dollop to the top of each cup. Garnish with a sprig of mint, grated chocolate, or a bite size candy bar and chill until party time.

Step 9: Make sure your serving platters are clean and ready to go.

Step 10: Arrange the napkins and plates near your serving area.

Step 11: Go freshen up.

TEN MINUTES BEFORE PARTY TIME

Step 1: Place tequila, margarita mix and a big bowl of ice within arms reach of The Magic Bullet.

Step 2: Pour the Clam Dip into a serving tray, add the crackers and chips to the tray and place in serving area near the napkins and plates.

Step 3: Heat the Cheese Dip for about one to one and a half minutes (until fully melted) and then pour into a serving platter or right over the top of a plate full of nachos.

Step 4: Place the Crock-Pot Hot Wings near the other serving trays (keep it plugged in) and lay tongs out next to the crock-pot.

Step 5: Go relax and wait for your guests.

45 MINUTES INTO THE GAME

Step 1: Start to boil a pot of water over high heat.

Step 2: Preheat your oven to 350 degrees.

Step 3: Go back and enjoy the game.

ONE HOUR INTO THE GAME

Step 1: Add the linguini noodles to the boiling water. Set a timer according to how long the package says to cook them.
Step 2: Put the loaves of garlic bread in the oven.
Step 3: Go back and enjoy the game.

10 OR SO MINUTES LATER

Step 1: Pour the Primavera Sauce into a large bowl, add the chopped vegetables, and heat in the microwave on high for 4-6 minutes.
Step 2: Check on the Fettuccine Noodles to see if they are done. When done, strain the Fettuccine Noodles in a colander, put them in a big serving bowl and toss with a tablespoon of olive oil.
Step3: Check the loaves of garlic bread. If they are warm and ready, turn the oven off but leave loaves inside.
Step 4: Pour the hot Primavera Sauce over the Fettuccini Noodles, toss a bit, and bring it to the serving area.
Step 5: Arrange the garlic bread onto a serving platter and put it next to the Pasta Primavera.
Step 6: Place the grated Parmesan cheese right next to the pasta, twist on the ***Shaker Lid*** and yell, "Come and get it!"

20 MINUTES AFTER DINNER

Step 1: Grind coffee beans and make a pot of coffee. Set it out with cream, sugar, spoons and cups.
Step 2: Place the chocolate mousse cups in the serving area with spoons and napkins, and let your guests know it's there.

The Fancy Brunch Party

This is a perfect gathering for family birthdays, graduation parties, and bridal or wedding showers. This is the type of affair Martha Stewart would be impressed by.

Guests Arrive to:
Ridiculously Quick Roasted Red Pepper Dip
Summer Salsa
Before You Can Say Olive Tapenade
Frozen Bellini Cocktails
Sparkling Water

First Course:
Gazpacho Shrimp Cocktail

Main Course:
Tomato Cheese Frittata
Mixed Green Salad with Spicy Avocado Dressing

Dessert:
Mixed Berry Sorbet
Cappuccino

SHOPPING LIST

Spices/Cooking/Jarred Foods Section

Splash of chicken (or vegetable) broth
Splash of balsamic vinegar (optional)
4 oz. salsa
1 can pitted black olives
1 can of anchovies (rinsed)
1 jar of roasted red peppers
1 jar of capers
1/2 cup extra virgin olive oil
1/4 cup balsamic vinegar

1 Tbs. Dijon mustard
Pinch of thyme
1/4 tsp. oregano
1/4 tsp. seasoned salt (optional)
1 cup of chicken stock
Splash of red wine vinegar
Salt and pepper
1/4 of a Hothouse (English) cucumber
Sprig of fresh chopped parsley

Dairy Section

1/2 cup of sour cream
4 eggs
Milk
2 oz. Cheddar cheese
Butter

Produce Section

6-8 cherry tomatoes (or 2 Roma or 1 regular-sized)
1 zucchini
1 cucumber
1 red pepper
3 sprigs fresh parsley
2 avocados
2 jalapeño peppers, seeded
3-4 boiler onion or 1 regular onion
20 cherry tomatoes or 3 regular-sized tomatoes
1 jar peeled garlic cloves
3 large bags of mixed salad greens
1 large box of mushrooms
1 bag of baby carrots

Beverages Section

Water
Orange juice

Coffee beans
Milk
Cinnamon
2-3 bags of ice

Frozen Foods Section
2 bags of frozen peaches
2 bags of frozen mixed berries
2 bags of frozen cooked baby shrimp

Bakery
3 French baguettes (or 3 loaves of Italian bread)

Dinnerware
3 8-inch square baking pans
20 small plates for dips
20-40 small cocktail napkins
20 cocktail cups for shrimp cocktail
20 cocktail cups for Bellini's
20 plates for main course
20 dinner-size napkins
20 cocktail cups for sorbet
20 coffee cups for cappuccinos

2 HOURS BEFORE THE PARTY

Step 1: Make a triple batch of the Roasted Red Pepper Dip by following the recipe on page 11 and chill in the refrigerator until party time.
Step 2: Make a triple batch of the Summer Salsa recipe on page 12 and chill in the refrigerator until party time.
Step 3: Make a triple batch of the Olive Tapenade by following the recipe on page 13. Chill in the refrigerator until party time.
Step 4: Defrost the frozen shrimp by running warm water over them for about 5 minutes. Put them in a strainer and jostle them every minute or so to thaw them evenly.

Step 5: Make a triple batch of the Gazpacho, by following the recipe on page 62 of the 10-Seconds or Less Cookbook. Then arrange the defrosted shrimp into the bottom of as many shrimp cocktail cups as you have guests. Pour the Gazpacho over the top to cover the shrimp. Chill the shrimp cocktail appetizers in the refrigerator.
Step 6: Rinse the salad greens under cold water and dry. Slice the mushrooms, julienne the baby carrots, and toss them into the salad greens. Chill in the refrigerator.
Step 7: Prepare a double batch of the Spicy Avocado Dressing by following the recipe on page 58.
Step 8: Make sure the serving platters for your dips are clean and place them in the serving area.
Step 9: Slice the loaves of French bread and store them in a sealed container until party time. (Most bakeries will slice them for you, a huge time savings!)
Step 10: Go relax and figure out what you're going to wear.

ONE HOUR BEFORE THE PARTY

Step 1: Mix 3 different colored batches of sorbet by following the recipe on page 74 of the 10 Second Recipes book. Then use a melon scoop and place 1 scoop of each color sorbet into as many cocktail cups as needed for your guests. Place the cups in the freezer until dessert time.
Step 2: Chop sprigs of mint to use as garnish, store in the refrigerator until dessert time.
Step 3: Make 3 batches of Tomato Cheese Frittata (do not cook) by following the recipe on page 34 and place in the refrigerator until party time.

15 MINUTES BEFORE THE PARTY

Step 1: Create your "cocktails station" by placing the ice, Bellini ingredients, cocktail glasses and ***Magic Bullet*** in the optimum location. (Bellini recipe is Page 47 of the 10-Second or Less Cookbook.)

Step 2: Arrange your dips and bread rounds in the proper serving platters.
Step 3: Prepare for your guests.

PARTY TIME!

Step 1: Greet your guests, and show them to the dips and the drink station (showing off your ***Magic Bullet!***). Be sure to offer a non-alcoholic beverage option, sparkling water and fresh juices are a nice choice.

25 MINUTES INTO THE PARTY

Step 1: Preheat the oven and cook the Frittatas.
Step 2: Ask if anyone needs a drink.

45 MINUTES INTO THE PARTY

Step 1: Serve the Gazpacho Shrimp Cocktail to your guests.
Step 2: Check the Frittatas.

1 HOUR INTO THE PARTY

Step 1: Check to see if the Frittatas are done. If so, remove from the oven and let cool for a bit while you do step 2.
Step 2: Toss the salad with the Spicy Avocado Dressing.
Step 3: Slice the Frittatas and place on a serving platter or onto individual plates.
Step 4: Set out the salad in a big bowl and allow guests to serve themselves.

1 HOUR FORTY MINUTES INTO THE PARTY

Step 1: Grind fresh coffee beans and brew a strong pot of coffee.
Step 2: Steam milk in the ***Tall Cup***. Pulse for a second or two, then heat in the microwave for 45 seconds.
Step 3: Serve the coffee.
Step 4: Serve the sorbet, adding the mint garnish.

The Magic Bullet Kids Birthday Bash

Just pick the theme, flowers or bugs, follow these instructions and sit back as you throw the cutest, most effortless birthday party you've ever seen! No child's birthday party should ever last longer than two hours. This will run about 1 1/2 to 2 hours, depending on the age of the children and how much time they spend on the activities.

Guests Arrive to:
Cream Cheese Cukes
Deviled Eggs
Veggie Platter with Ranch Dressing

Activity #1
Flower Girl Seed Planting
Or
Bug Refrigerator Magnets

Main Course:
Egg Salad, Chicken Salad and Deviled Ham Puzzle Sandwiches
Sweet and Sour Meatballs
Ham and Cheese Mini Quiches

Activity #2:
Make Your Own Dirt Cake
Dessert:
Eat Your Dirt Cake
Drinks:
Juice Boxes
Bottled Water

Stand by Activity:
The Secret Garden (telephone)
Caterpillar (Flower Power) Conga Line

SHOPPING LIST

Dairy Section
Cream cheese
4 oz. buttermilk
24 eggs
Cheddar Cheese
1/2 gallon of heavy cream

Produce Section
Chives
1 garlic clove
1 green onion
1 regular onion
1 sprig flat-leaf parsley
Pineapple
Celery
2 fresh basil leaves
2 fresh chives
1 small pepper
Carrot sticks
Celery sticks
1 bag of cherry tomatoes

Spices/Baking Section
Oregano
Salt
Black pepper
Paprika
Brown sugar
Hershey's™ chocolate syrup
2 package of gummy worms
1 package of coconut
Green food coloring
Plastic flowers or gummy bugs

1 package of mini candy bars.
1/3 cup bread crumbs
1 tsp. parsley flakes

Sauces/Canned Food Section
1 jar of mayonnaise
Mustard
Sweet pickle relish
Hot red pepper sauce
Chicken Broth
Vinegar
Soy sauce
2 12- or 14-oz. cans of pineapple chunks (save 2 slices for the Cream Cheese Cukes)

Meat Section
Ham
Chicken
1/2 lb. ground beef (or turkey)

Refrigerator Section
24 mini quiche shells (or mini Fillo Shells)

Cookies Section
1 package Oreo cookies

Miscellaneous
8 small terra cotta pots or 8 clear plastic cups

THREE WEEKS BEFORE THE PARTY

Step 1: Decide if it's a kids-only, or kids and parents party and prepare accordingly (for 3-5 year olds you'll need one adult for every four children, 6 to 8 years – one adult per 6 kids).
Step 2: Send out invitations with an RSVP number.

Step 3: Purchase the items for Activity #1 and the stand by activity of your choice.
Step 4: Purchase gift bags for the guests (optional, but very popular) and items for inside the gift bags (many websites specialize in birthday party gift bags and decorations).

1 WEEK BEFORE THE PARTY

Step 1: Buy 20 cups, 20 small plates, 20 entrée plates, 20 forks, 20 spoons
Step 2: Purchase any decorations (balloons, flower theme stuff, bug theme stuff) to decorate the party area.

1 DAY BEFORE THE PARTY

Step 1: Purchase everything on the shopping list.
Step 2: Make sure you have everything you need for the activities.
Step 3: Make a double batch of Deviled Eggs by following the recipe on Page 20 and let them chill overnight in the refrigerator (you can lay them out on a cookie sheet and cover them with wax paper).

5 HOURS BEFORE PARTY TIME

Step 1: Make a triple batch of meatballs (Recipe page 77) and a triple batch of Sweet and Sour Sauce (Recipe page 62-63), and put them both in a crock-pot. Stir them together and cook on high for about 4-5 hours.

2 HOURS BEFORE THE PARTY

Step 1: Make a double batch of Cream Cheese Cukes by following the recipe on page 23 (we found pineapple to be the preferred "add-in" for the toddler crowd). Chill in the refrigerator until party time.
Step 2: Make a triple batch of the Ranch Dressing, recipe on page 57.
Step 3: Make 15-20 mini quiches by following the recipe on page 39-40. Instead of pouring the egg mixture in the big pie shell, use the mini shells or create mini quiche shells out of fillo dough. Bake

them now, they'll be perfectly delicious at room temperature come party time.
Step 4: Make 15-20 Sandwich Puzzles by following these instructions:

Sandwich Puzzles

First ... Make triple batches of Egg Salad, Deviled Ham and Chicken Salad by following the recipes from page 64-66 of the Magic Bullet 10-Second or Less Recipe Book.
Next ... Smear the sandwich spread on the inside of 2 pieces of white or wheat bread.

Notes

If you are using really soft bread, you may want to wait until 30 minutes before the party to build the puzzle sandwiches. That way, you don't have to worry about the puzzles being soggy.

Then ... Take a cookie cutter (flower or bug theme) and press it down into the center of the sandwich until it's separated. Then, use a knife to cut straight lines from the edge of the flower or bug cut out, to the crust. (For little ones, 3-4 pieces are plenty. Cut into more pieces for larger kids.)
Finally ... Mix up the pieces from one sandwich on a small plate and repeat for each sandwich.

Step 5: Follow the recipe for the Dirt Cake on page 83-84, but don't build the cake…keep all of the elements separate, because each child is going to build their own dirt cake.
Step 6: Set up for Activity #1. Get all of the elements situated.
Step 7: Decorate the party area.
Step 8: Find the serving platters you'll need and make sure they are clean and ready to go.
Step 9: Check on the meatballs. Give them a stir and if they look cooked, turn them down to the low setting.
Step 10: Relax and then get ready.

ONE HOUR BEFORE THE PARTY

Step 1: Check on the meatballs. Stir them and if you haven't turned them down to the low setting already, do so now.

15 MINUTES BEFORE THE PARTY

Step 1: Place the Cream Cheese Cukes, Deviled Eggs and Veggie Platter (Carrot, Celery Sticks, Cherry Tomatoes) with Ranch Dressing out in the serving area.
Step 2: Put the juice boxes and waters out in an accessible area.
Step 3: Stir the meatballs.

PARTY TIME!

Step 1: Greet your guests; show them to the serving area.
Step 2: Once the majority of the guests have arrived, start activity #1.

FORTY MINUTES INTO THE PARTY

Step 1: While the kids are finishing Activity #1, place the meatballs, quiches and puzzle sandwiches in a serving area and let the party goers know they can "Come and get it!"
Step 2: As the kids are eating, get ready for the Dirt Cake Activity. Get everything laid out and ready to go.
Step 3: When the kids are done eating invite them over to the dirt cake area and explain how it works (see explanation below).
Step 4: Let the kids eat their dirt cakes.

ONE HOUR 15 MINUTES INTO THE PARTY

Step 1: Clean up the kids.
Step 2: Either open gifts, or roll into the Standby Activity.

ONE HOUR 45 MINUTES INTO THE PARTY

Step 1: Sing the goodbye song and show everyone to the door.
Step 2: Make your favorite frozen cocktail and put your feet up!

The Activities

Flower Girl Seed Planting (assuming 8 guests)
Have each guest plant their seeds by lining the bottom of the pot with rocks for draining, adding soil, seeds and water. Then they decorate the top of a wide Popsicle stick with their name in glitter, and stick it in their plant as a stake.

8 terra cotta plant pots
Bag of pebbles (enough to line the bottom of each pot)
15 wide Popsicle sticks
Soil (enough to fill the 8 pots)
2-3 packets of seeds
12 pack of thin colored markers
2-3 bottles of glue
Multi-colored glitter
8 plastic trowels

Bug Refrigerator Magnets (assuming 8 guests)
Have the kids cut out a felt "base" for their bugs. Then have them glue on pom-poms, eyes, antennas etc. When they are done, add a strip of magnetic tape to the backside of the bug's felt and...it's a magnet!

20-30 small pom-poms
20-30 wiggly eyes
20-30 pipe cleaners
Several colored squares of felt
Whatever else you can think of

Flower/Dirt Cake Activity (for 8)
This cake can be tweaked just a bit to be perfect for girls or boys. For girls, top each "flower pot" with a plastic flower. For boys, add gummy bugs and green coconut grass to the dirt cake and you are sure to get a million giggles.

Depending on the seating arrangement (you want all ingredients to be within arms reach of your guests) you'll want either 2-4 "cake stations". Each station will have a bowl of Oreo dirt, "mud" (chocolate mousse), gummy worms, "grass" green coconut and either plastic flowers (for girls) or gummy bugs (for boys and cool tomboys). See recipe on page 83-84.

Secret Garden (Telephone Game)
Need:

12 slips of paper (flowery is best)
One decorative bag or bowl

The Game:
This back up activity is a stand by in case you need to entertain the group. This glorified game of telephone is fun and easy. Simply write about 12 (one for each guest with some spares) age-appropriate, garden-related statements ("A rose by any other name smells as sweet" or "Roses are red, violets are blue") and place them in a bag or bowl. (Use fancy, flowery paper and decorate a gift bag with flowers if you want.) Have the kids sit in a circle, let the birthday girl go first and pick a "statement" out of the bag. She whispers to the friend on her right, then each child whispers it to the next around the circle until it comes back to the child just left of the birthday girl. That child says the statement out loud. The next turn goes to the child to the right of the birthday girl, and so on until everyone has had a turn.

Caterpillar (Flower Power) Conga Line
Need:
One pair of deely-boppers (head-band with bug-like antennas on it). Music that can be started and stopped easily (buggy music is the best).

The Game:
The birthday boy (or girl) puts on the deely-bopper, and the kids line up in a Conga Line. The music starts and the Caterpillar dances around the room until the music stops. At that time, the first in line hands the "antennas" to the next in line and the music starts again, and so on until everyone gets a turn.

To make this work with the flower theme, simply swap out the deely-boppers with a flowery hat.

Get a FREE Magic Bullet!

Now's your chance to take home a complete Magic Bullet System for ***FREE***! Just go to the official Magic Bullet website at ***www.BuyTheBullet.com*** and find out how becoming a valued Magic Bullet customer entitles you to the chance to take home an entire Magic Bullet system – a nearly $100 value — ***ABSOLUTELY FREE***!

Go to www.BuyTheBullet.com Right Now!

While you're there, be sure to check out these other valuable opportunities:

Special Insider Discounts

As a Homeland Housewares preferred customer, you'll receive special discounts on additional Magic Bullets and Magic Bullet accessories. Throwing a party? Take advantage of your preferred customer status for special discounts on 6-packs of our ever-popular Party Mugs, or the new Magic Bullet Chopper which turns your Magic Bullet into a full-sized food processor for making delicious treats like creamy Killer Coleslaw and a zesty Carrot Ginger Salad that will knock your socks off, all in just seconds.

Even More Fantastic Magic Bullet Recipes

The Homeland Housewares staff is constantly creating new and exciting Magic Bullet recipes. We regularly post new Bullet discoveries, seasonal favorites and traditional Holiday Recipes that are absolutely delicious and unbelievably easy.

The Magic Bullet Recipe Exchange

Because the Magic Bullet is all about experimenting, we've created a forum where you can share your culinary masterpieces with other Bulleteers. New, innovative and unbelievably tasty recipes are posted every day. A wonderful place to share and learn...you'll definitely want to bookmark this page!

Even More Step-By-Step Party Guides

Check out the Bullet Buffet step-by-step party planner that includes a shopping list, party tips, serving suggestions and more. And how about a Bullet Barbeque? Come one, come all and see why the Magic Bullet truly is — hands down — the Ultimate Party machine.

Special Offers on Other Homeland Housewares Products

As a preferred Homeland Housewares customer, you will receive special offers on the entire line of exciting Homeland Housewares products designed to make life easy... at home.

Go to www.BuyTheBullet.com Right Now!

Recipe Favorites:

Recipe Favorites: